GOOD
VITTLES

GOOD VITTLES

One Man's Meat,
a Few Vegetables,
and a Drink or Two

A.D. LIVINGSTON

Lyons & Burford, Publishers

Printed in the United States of America
10 9 8 7 6 5 4 3 2 1

Library of Congress Cataloging-in-Publication Data

Livingston, A. D., 1932–
    Good vittles : one man's meat, a few vegetables, and a drink or two / A.D. Livingston.
    p.   cm.
    Includes index.
    ISBN 1-55821-079-2 (pbk.) : $13.95
    1. Cookery.   I. Title.
TX714.L59 1990
641.5—dc20   90-42744
                                    CIP

For Helen, Ginger, Kathleen

and the rest of our good womenfolks everywhere

CONTENTS

A Few Vegetables

A Drink or Two

ACKNOWLEDGMENTS

Parts of this book were first published, in slightly different form, in the pages of *Outdoor Life*, *Field & Stream*, and *Sports Afield* magazines. Also, parts of two chapters were reprinted in Outdoor Life Book Club's *Freshwater Fishing Yearbook* and *Deer Hunter's Yearbook*. Further acknowledgment must be made to my *Outdoor Life's Complete Fish & Game Cookbook*, not for quotes, but for similarity in recipes on frying fish and cooking "indoor barbecue."

I need to thank my friends Dan Webster, Greg Rane, Carl Barber, and Bill Parker for their culinary advice and instigation.

GOOD
VITTLES

FOREWORD

I'm not a well-travelled man. It's true that, on a modest budget, I have enjoyed a menu or two in France, although, owing to a slight speech impediment, I had great difficulty in pronouncing those curious French sounds. I once enjoyed a loaf of bread, a ball of cheese, and a bottle of wine on a seawall somewhere in Sicily. I ate a kabob, rather hastily, on a sidewalk in Algeria.

In my own country, I have eaten in a number of restaurants, from old Cuban establishments in Ybor City to lobster houses in Boston and back down to New Orleans. Once I headed West, but I turned around at El Paso. Maybe I'll go back one day. Each season I enjoy the soft white roe of mullet from the Gulf of Mexico, and one of my favorite eating spots is Seafood Unlimited, an oyster bar with only 6 stools, in an alley just off the square in Abbeville, Alabama. You have to squeeze into this place. The stool on the far end puts you at too acute an angle to watch the television screen, and, on the other end of the counter, the cash register takes up too much room, making it difficult to fit in a tray of oysters, crackers, and hot sauce.

Perhaps I shall travel in my old age. But I won't go all the way to Moscow for a McDonald's hamburger, and I'm not likely to drink a Budweiser beer in a Dublin pub. I would love to feast on an iguana in Central America. A leg of lamb in Afghanistan. A domestic duck in Canton. I could spend a season learning about the caribou cookery in Lapland. Maybe I'll go to Vermont during maple syrup time, mainly because I'm curious to see whether the Yankees actually eat the syrup as thin as they bottle it and market it to the world. If they do, I'll leave them with it and head to coastal Carolina for some thick cane syrup for sopping with my breakfast biscuits.

But I don't *have* to travel anywhere for culinary adventure. In my own kitchen, with a few simple ingredients, I can turn out better steaks than I have eaten publicly in Kansas City and other places. Better drinks than I have found in the bars of Manhattan. Part of the pleasure of cooking, of course, is in preparing a good dish of meat, a few vegetables, and a drink or two for someone other than one's self. To this end, I lean toward perfection of technique instead of toward a long list of secret or esoteric stuff.

As a glance through this book will show, some of my favorite dishes require only 3 or 4 ingredients. Whether or not such a sparse list constitutes a real recipe, and, by extension, whether or not this little text is really a cookbook, may be open to question. After all, one or two of the chapters don't contain a single recipe. When I do set forth a long list, I try hard to have all of it in one place rather than send the reader scurrying to other parts of the work. I confess that a full defense of such a radical departure from other cookbooks would have to be lengthy, and, in the end, I would have to reveal that I, rather innocently, set out to write not a cookbook but a collection of loosely connected essays and fun pieces on food and drink.

But writing such a book is one thing, and marketing it to the world is another. Somebody, after all, has got to pay the printer and the bookbinder. In the end, prudence prevailed, and I am pleased to loose my little work in the traffic of the booktrade under the guise of *Good Vittles*. If it finds a few readers and makes their daily fare and its preparation a little more enjoyable, draws a chuckle or two, or provokes a reply, then the effort won't have been wasted.

—A.D. Livingston

PART 1
Meat

HOW TO FRY FISH

I don't care what my wife says. I was *not* shouting at the woman. How she and T-Bone McClenney choose to cook fish in the privacy of their own kitchen is their business, not mine.

What we had that night in their lakefront home was a controlled disagreement on the proper way to salt fish before frying them, and the woman had some peculiar notions, to say the least. She did, however, agree that salting fish ahead of time tends to draw the water out of the meat. She further agreed that demoisturization is partly a function of time.

"That's why," she said, nodding toward 17 salted crappies lined up neatly on the counter, "you're supposed to point them North and South for a while before you fry them."

Her grandfather, a Georgia Cracker, had taught her to "polarize" fish and he, she said, fried the best crappie she had ever put into her mouth, only he called them white perch. I didn't refute her statement and, during dinner, it was T-Bone McClenney who hinted that her fried fish were not exactly the best in the world.

"You know," he said, lackadaisically pulling the dorsal fins from a crappie, "the best fish I ever ate came out of the Choctawhatchee River back home."

He was speaking of a small steam in southeast Alabama, where we were born and raised. Only he was from across the river and sometimes fished the West Choctawhatchee in Dale County as well as the East Fork in Henry County.

My wife turned a little red in the face and said that the Pea River and the Pea Creek fish up in Barbour County were hard to beat. The argument that developed was moot, really, since the Pea and the Choctawhatchee run together a few miles below the Florida line. In my opinion, you've got to get up into Crackerneck on the East Choctawhatchee before you can tell much difference, and the plain truth is that fish from these streams aren't a whole lot better than fish from clean streams in Georgia, Vermont, Arizona, South Dakota, Northern California, Hawaii, or even Arkansas.

The crappies on the table that night had been taken from the deep, cool waters of central Florida's Lake Weir, and they were just as good—or should have been. The difference was in the way the fish were cooked.

Over the years, the authors (and editors) of cookbooks and magazine articles have modified our basic recipes. Feeling a need to change a recipe for one reason or another, legal or otherwise, the easiest course was to add something to the list of ingredients. A pinch of this, a squirt of that. Advertising managers have also influenced our cooking, and many an editor's arm has been twisted enough to throw in a drop or two of Worcestershire sauce or some such stuff, depending on what was being advertised in a particular magazine issue. Once inserted into a list, the ingredient tends to stay. The result is that some recipes coming from New York and New Orleans these days have an ingredients list a mile and a half long. In any case, I've tried dozens of recipes over the years for fried fish, but I've gone back to basics, looking for the old values, and here's what I recommend:

The World's Best Fried Fish

fresh fish
cooking oil
white corn meal, fine
salt

Let me say, first, that I have sometimes enjoyed fish fried with more elaborate ingredients. For instance, you can dip the fish in whisked chicken egg and roll them in all manner of things to make a thick batter. That's good. But I prefer the taste of fish, and I don't see the advantage of a thick batter if you've got enough fish to feed everybody. Moreover, I might add, health food freaks will surely acknowledge that a thick batter soaks up lots of grease.

Although my recipe is simple, it is important to use the right kind of oil and meal. I prefer peanut oil because it can be heated to a high temperature before it starts to smoke and because it is relatively odorless and tasteless. The meal that I use is white and finely ground. It is almost as fine as flour, whereas some of the coarse corn meals are gritty to the touch. There are a number of brands of fine ground corn meal in local grocery stores in my area, and they are usually identified as "stone ground" or "water ground style."

I'm not writing a treatise on corn meal at this time, but I'll have to repeat what a fellow named Pete Nowell once said to me: "Some of this new hybrid corn is so hard that the weevils won't eat it. Any kernel of corn that is too hard for a weevil to bore is too hard to make good corn bread." I also read, in *The Foxfire Book*, further advice on what might well be a related matter: "Do not use a hybrid or yellow corn. Use a good, fresh, pure white corn like Holcomb Prolific which will produce about three quarts of whiskey per bushel." For cooking purposes, it may be important to note that most people think the term "water ground" is the key to good meal. In truth, not much meal these days is ground by water power, although it may be ground in between stones and is available in coarse, medium, fine, and extra fine grinds. The unspoken key here is the fact that so-called "water ground" corn meal is made from corn that has not been leached out in water and then baked before grinding. It still contains the "germ," and bread made from it might properly be called whole-corn bread. "Water ground" corn meal is made from unprocessed corn. I have, in fact, taken shucked corn to a mill and had it ground by a fellow who wore a folded handkerchief over his nose and had white corn dust in his hair and beard. Using whole and un-processed corn is, in my opinion, more important than color. (I might also point out that some people swear by purple or Indian corn meal, which is available in some parts of the southwest.) Before leaving the subject, let me add that, for whatever reasons, some meal for sale in super-markets, usually yellow, is simply too hard and too gritty for use in the recipe above.

Once you get the right corn meal and the proper cooking oil, the real secret to frying good fish is in careful attention to detail. Here's my method:

Catch your own fish and dress them soon after pulling them out of the water. For best results, cook them fresh. (If you freeze them, make sure they are covered in water; that is, frozen in blocks of ice.) Whether you fillet or pan dress depends on personal preference and, to some degree, on how large the fish are and where they were caught. A three-pound bass from a mud-bottomed pond, for instance, should probably be filleted instead of pan dressed and skinned instead of scaled. And some fish require neither scaling or skinning. Any small brook trout or a 7-inch chan-nel catfish from swift waters can be fried, to advantage, with the skin on.

When the fish are ready to cook, fill a frying pan or deep-fat fryer with a least 1¼ inches of oil. Deeper oil works better. Heat the oil almost to the smoking point—the hotter the better, within reason. Frying fish fast keeps the juices in and the grease out. I heat the oil on high and then reduce the heat slightly just before I cook, and I make adjustments all along.

While the oil is heating, salt a few fish to taste, sprinkling both sides. Then meal the fish. Mealing works best if the fish are quite moist but not dripping. The fish can be rolled in meal, but I prefer to shake them with the meal in a paper bag or a plastic container. Heavy-duty sugar bags are ideal for this, and I also like the heavy brown bags that supermarkets use to put ice cream in.

After mealing, place the fish in the hot oil. I use tongs. While the first batch is cooking (just a few minutes) salt another batch and shake in meal. Turn the fish in the pan with tongs and brown the other side. Do not overcook. A rule of thumb: When a fish or fillet floats in the oil, it is ready to be taken out. The exact cooking time depends on the size and thickness of the piece as well as on the temperature of the oil.

As soon as the fish are done, drain them on absorbent paper. This is very important, especially when you are cooking a large batch. I use brown paper from ordinary grocery bags. In fact, we often serve the fish on these bags. Actually, I usually drain the fish on one bag while I cook another batch. Then I move them to a fresh bag.

Eat the fish while they are hot.

All we serve with fried fish, usually, is bread, fresh sliced tomatoes (or a salad), french fries, and iced tea. We always have corn bread, which should be cooked before the fish, or at the same time in a separate frying pan. Again, I prefer simple ingredients for corn bread:

Livingston's Corn Bread

white corn meal, fine
good water
salt

I pour the meal into a bowl and add salt to taste. Stir in warm water until the mixture is the right consistency to spoon into the frying pan. I usually let the dough sit for 10 or 15 minutes and then add a bit more water to get the right texture. If the dough is too soupy, the bread will flatten out in the pan; if it's too thick, the bread will be too dry.

Using a greased tablespoon, drop golf-ball-size dollops into about an inch of hot peanut oil—not quite so hot as for the fish. Cook the bread a little slower; otherwise, it will burn on the outside before the inside gets done. Some people add onions to their corn bread and call the result hush-puppies, which is fine if you like onions in your corn bread. Others have a big thing about mixing the meal with the beer instead of water. It tastes good but, in my opinion, it's better to drink the beer while you are frying the corn bread and the fish.

So there you have it—the world's best fish recipe. Deviate from the simple ingredients list and the cooking instructions at your culinary peril. Seriously, try to avoid two common causes of unpalatable fried fish: (1) Do not overcook. Cooking too long on low heat results in dry, chewy fish. (2) Do not pile the fried fish onto a platter without draining them properly.

I must admit at this time that the Lake Weir crappies at T-Bone McClenney's house were pretty good, in spite of the fact that they weren't salted properly. At least the top of the batch was good. The woman—and I didn't say a word about it—made terrible mistake No. 2. She removed the fish from the frying pan and piled them directly onto a serving platter without proper draining. By the time we finished the meal, there must have been a quarter of an inch of grease in the bottom of the platter. And fried fish sitting in grease will surely be greasy, no matter whether you point them North, South, East, or West.

Late one summer afternoon, some years later, the smell of frying fish came wafting through my yard (along with the sound of squalling cats) and I followed my nose to Dan ⎪ *10*

Webster's place, just down the street. He was frying a batch of bluegills in his backyard, and he had quite a rig for it. A large rectangular iron container, which must have held four or five gallons of peanut oil, sat on an angle iron frame just over a series of gas burners, fueled by a portable butane tank. Some farmer had drained a fish pond and Dan had made away with a tubful of large bluegills and a 9-pound bass. He still had the fish heads, which in turn had drawn some neighborhood tomcats into the bushes on a vacant lot between our houses. When I arrived, Dan was cooking the bluegills, and I decided to watch for a while, just to see if he knew what he was doing. There must have been 15 cats over in the bushes on the vacant lot, who also took an interest in the proceedings. For some reason, however, they kept their distance.

So far as I could tell, Dan had everything about right, except that he used Hall's meal whereas I use Adam's. The heat was perfect, and the fish were being drained properly, first in a strainer, and then on brown paper. After finishing the fish, Dan started on some cornbread, and he had two batches made up in order to settle an argument that he was having with Miss Ginger Reeves. One batch was pretty basic, and the other batch, called hushpuppies, had chicken egg and some milk and baking powder and other stuff in it. After the bread was ready, Dan then cooked some French fries.

Well, I ate seven or eight of the bluegills, along with a few mouthfuls of bread and potatoes, and I'll have to allow that they were quite fitting, although Dan had made a peculiar cut in the side of the fish when he gutted them, and, of course, one batch of bread had too much stuff in it. And the potatoes had been peeled.

"*All* of it was good, Dan," I said, taking a napkin and wiping the corners of my mouth. "But you cooked it exactly backwards."

He stared at me and waited for me to explain myself.

"You cooked the fish first, then the bread, and then the potatoes," I explained. "You ought to have started with the potatoes, then the bread, then the fish. You ought to have cooked the bluegill last so that they won't get cold while you're doing the potatoes and bread."

"You're a damned frying pan cook," he said, shaking some long outdoor chef's tongs at me. "Get yourself a real fish cooker like this and it won't take you an hour and a half to fry ten or twelve batches of stuff. Hell, man, I'm already eating before you ever finish cooking. Moreover," he continued, "the Websters have always cooked the potatoes last because they absorb the fish taste and the odor, leaving the peanut oil as fresh and as good as new. Then, after everything cools down and the dredgings settle, you pour off the oil and put it back into a jug until the next time you want to fry."

Well, ol' Dan had me for a while, so I took another bluegill or two.

"Just feel free to help yourself," he said. "If the fish aren't too cold to suit you."

"Why thank you, Dan," I said. "Yes sir, these here sure are good bluegill. But I think maybe you ought to try straining the peanut oil through some of those coffee filters when you're *finished* cooking. Then, the next time around, you can fry the potatoes first to get out whatever smell the filter might have missed from the previous cooking. Then proceed with the bread. Then fry the fish last, where they'll be right hot. It's not any of my business, but——"

"That's exactly right," Dan said. The tomcats had started squalling around in the bushes on the vacant lot, and Dan threw them a handful of bluegill heads to hush them.

At about that time, Miss Ginger Reeves came out of the house, just as pretty as she could be, with some sliced Vidalia onions, luscious red tomatoes, and crinkle-cut cucumber pickles. And some iced tea.

I took a glass of the tea, made, I noticed, with square ice, | *12* and I sampled a few slices of onions and tomatoes, along with a pickle or two.

"Why don't you eat with us, A.D.?" Miss Ginger asked.

"He's already eaten," Dan said. Then he looked at me, waved me off, and added, "Just feel free to drop in again at any time."

"Thank you, Miss Ginger," I said, ignoring Dan. "I would love to sit for a while, but I had better get on back home so I can write down this wonderful hushpuppy recipe before I forget it." I popped another one into my mouth, chewed on it, and considered its qualities. "I'll swear, these hushpuppies beseem publication. They sure do crunch better than those ol' mushy things that Dan Webster mixed up!"

Dan picked up a fish head to throw at me, but I made it around the corner of the house before he let it go.

HOW TO BROIL A STEAK

During the great race for the moon in the 1960's, a red-headed editor at a NASA documentation center where I worked asked for my advice on which kind of beefsteak to buy. She had come to this federal outpost from New York City, where, she said, she had worked as an editor for a major publisher and had met Bennett Cerf. I won't try to hide my dislike for the woman, but it's simply not true that I asked why she didn't stay in New York. In fact, I went out of my way to avoid a fuss with her. The plain truth is that she had a problem with the facts. I too had met Cerf and I had even published a novel with a New York outfit. In any case, the tandem colon setup was unfortunate, and I would take it all back if I could. Here's what happened:

Shortly after she came in from New York, slashing left and right with a blue pencil, she edited a résumé that I had prepared for an official NASA document. At one point in the text, I had written 'F.. Kline.' She circled the two periods in 'F.. Kline' and made a snide remark in the margin. Drawing my own pencil, I demanded that she defend her marks. She launched into a windy discourse about the proper notation for the ellipsis mark, saying that it must contain at least three periods, '. . .' or four, '. . . .' if the ellipsis ended a sentence. And the marks, she went on, always had a space between them, '. . .' and were not jammed up like my '..' notation.

Knowing all that, I said, "Excuse me, madame, but the mark was not intended to denote ordinary ellipsis."

"Well what, pray tell, was it intended to denote?" she asked, louder than necessary. All the other editors and writers quit the moon race to listen in.

"It's a tandem colon," I said.

"A what?"

"A tandem colon," I said.

"A *what?*" She acted as though she couldn't believe her ears.

"A tandem colon," I explained, "is a mark that, according to *Webster's Second New International Dictionary of the English Language*, is used in abbreviations to distinguish between males and females. Thus, 'F.. Kline' with the two periods, or tandem colon, denotes a female, usually spelled Frances, whereas 'F. Kline' with one period, denotes a male, usually spelled Francis." (I might add that the tandem colon was dropped from the newer *Webster's Third*.)

Quickly the woman glanced around to see how many people were listening in. Everybody was. A long silence followed, during which period she turned white and the Russians jumped ahead of us a notch or two in the race for the moon.

When everyone had eagerly returned to their own work, she got up and nonchalantly walked back to the podium, on which sat the huge *Webster's Second*. She turned deep into the book, at about where the T's ought to be. Before long, she put her finger on an entry—and her face turned as red as her hair. I didn't look at her any longer, but shortly I heard her returning to her desk. Without a word she came, sat down, and buried herself in a NASA document.

Several weeks later, having heard of my dinner parties atop Pea Ridge, near Skin'um, Tennessee, she asked for my advice on beefsteak. Being a southern gentlemen, I held back my reservations about her method of cooking a steak. In all honesty, I simply didn't care how they cooked steak or used tandem colons in New York. Or in Texas, for that matter. To answer her question, however, I said that I was just a country bumpkin, but, in my humble opinion, a T-bone or a porterhouse about 2 inches thick was the only steak to buy. Quickly she pointed out that she and her husband, a mathematician, had a small child, and that their family unit didn't *need* three T-bone steaks 2 inches thick, and certainly not three porterhouse steaks 2 inches thick. And there was, she went on, no equitable way to divide two T-bones or two porterhouses among three people, whereas a sirloin could be cut most any way, as needed.

She had a point. Still, she had asked me for my opinion and I gave it to her. Something about the way I said it must have ticked her off, however, and I noticed that four or five other writers and editors had started listening in, and one of them, something of a poet, looked straight at me over little half glasses on his nose.

Quickly I changed the subject, asking if anyone knew why ducks have flat feet. Nobody knew. "For stomping out forest fires!" I said, speaking to the company, straining hard to add some cheer to the workplace.

"That's sick," she said, "and, since you presume to be a writer, you should know that there is no such word as 'stomp.' The correct verb is 'stamp.'"

"Well," I said, "a school marm might *stamp* her foot to gain the attention of her class or a redheaded editor might *stamp* out a tandem colon, but a cowboy *stomps* on rattlesnakes and a duck *stomps* out forest fires. And anybody," I added, "with good taste and common sense prefers T-bone to sirloin, at least for broiling steak the famous A.D. Livingston way."

"And your method of broiling," she said, "messes up the oven."

"Well," I said, "that's not my problem."

That statement really ticked her off. She called me a name or two, got up, and stamped out in her high heeled shoes. But, of course, she did raise a good point. My method of broiling *will* mess up an oven.

In any case, family-type, budget-minded people have, I think, influenced the average thickness of the American T- | *16* bone. These days, most meat is cut, wrapped, and put out for sale in neat units. In order to sell more T-bones, the butcher has made them thinner and thinner. My guess is that your average T-bone these days is down to ¾-inch, and getting even thinner by the decade.

How thick *should* the steak be? Some experts say 2 inches. I've said it myself. But I suspect that more people give this specification than practice it. And I'll have to admit that a 2-inch thick T-bone is really more steak than most modern people want or need, and, furthermore, such a thick piece is not ideal for the type of broiling that I practice and recommend. I'll take one exactly 1¼ inches thick, if I can get it that way.

Frankly, most people are going to buy whatever steaks that the meat department of the local supermarket puts out for sale, and will not often ask a butcher to cut the meat to exact measure. This is especially true in the larger markets, which sell motor oil and mouse traps and fold-up lawn chairs in addition to T-bones. Ask a clerk for a special cut, and you'll get, first, a look of "My God, Mac, we've got a thousand pieces of meat already cut and wrapped. Why can't you eat one of them?" But if you persist, you can often get pretty much what you want. You'll have to wait, of course, and may even have to come back the next day. If you want to push your luck, ask for steaks that have a good portion of "tenderloin" as well as what I call "top loin."

Let me explain. If you gnaw all the meat off two T-bone steaks of similar size and butt the big ends of the bones together, you'll have a cross-section of the backbone. You'll even see the hole (or two half holes) that contained the bone marrow. The meat on the top of the cross section is from the "backstrap" or "top loin." The meat on the bottom section, always smaller than the top, is from the "tenderloin" section. It follows, I think, that a T-bone with a large portion of tenderloin is desirable. (The same is true of pork chops.)

Some years ago, one of my dinner guests, the daughter of a rich doctor, said that my steaks presented something of a dilemma for her. She wanted to save the small part for last because it was better; but if she didn't eat it right away, it got cold while she was working on the top part. I couldn't help the poor girl. We all have our problems, and it's a rough, tough life. In short, it's hard to have your tenderloin and eat it too.

At one extreme, the T-bones steaks with very small tenderloin rounds are cut from next to what I call rib steaks, and there is a fine line, in the butcher's eye, where a T-bone stops being a T-bone and becomes something else. By the same token, the T-bones with large tenderloin rounds are cut from a section next to porterhouse steaks, and there is a fine line where a T-bone turns into porterhouse. The porterhouse, of course, is a very good piece of meat, but you don't often see one in most supermarkets. Maybe the butchers save them for themselves or for fancy restaurants, most of which don't know how to cook them to advantage. In any case, both the porterhouse and the T-bone are choice cuts of meat for broiling because their texture is just right. As a rule of thumb, any muscle that is used constantly is tougher than one that is not much used. Thus, any muscle running along the backbone is more tender than any muscle in the legs.

I have broiled steaks successfully in a gas oven (or under a broiling unit in the bottom of a gas oven) but I really prefer electrical heat for this method of cooking. Further, I want the heat *over* the meat instead of under it. With prime steak, usually T-bone or porterhouse, what I'm after is the flavor of the meat, not the flavor of smoke or burnt grease. To be sure, I truly enjoy smoked meat and expertly charbroiled meat, but, if I be honest about it, I have to say that oven broiled steak is better, at least to me, in both flavor and juiciness.

Consider what happens. If the meat is directly *over* the heat, the bottom cooks first and the juices drip down onto the coals or heating element. But if the meat is directly *under* the heat, the top cooks first and the juices drain down into the meat itself. Before the juices from the top drain all the way through, the steak is turned over, and the juices flow the other way. When cooked medium rare, which is what I recommend, almost all of the juices are served up with the steak. (In order to retain the juices, some people sear a steak in a very hot frying pan, or on a griddle, before cooking it further. I seldom do this, partly because it seems to make the surface of the meat a little leathery.)

Further, the surface of the meat should be quite close to the heating coils. I recommend 2 inches, measuring from the *top* of the meat. The problem here is that the slide-out racks in most ovens are adjustable only in rather large steps. This is further complicated if you have to allow for the thickness of the broiling pan and the thickness of the meat. But try for 2 inches. Anyhow, here's all you need in order to cook the world's best steak.

A.D.'s Pepper T-bone

T-bone or porterhouse steaks
crushed black pepper (coarse)
salt

Put some peppercorns into a clean piece of cloth and beat it with a hammer or some other tool until they are crushed. I like to use a heavy cast iron shoe tool that belonged to my grandfather. It is slightly curved, and it crushes the pepper with a tilting or rolling motion instead of a pounding motion. (Some folks use a rolling pin.) You can also buy coarsely ground black pepper at the supermarket, or you can use a mill, adjusted for a coarse grind. I usually crush mine. Either way, the aroma of the freshly crushed pepper is wonderful.

After you get a goodly amount of pepper, lay your steaks out on a smooth surface and sprinkle each one generously. With your fingers or the palm part of your thumb, press the pepper into the meat. Turn the steaks and press some pepper into the other side. Let the steaks sit for at least 20 minutes.

When you are ready to cook, preheat the oven broiler for a few minutes. Then place the steaks onto a broiling pan directly under and about 2 inches away from the heating coils. Leave the oven door *open* while the steak cooks. Broil the steaks for 5 minutes on one side, then turn with tongs. (Always use tongs for turning a steak; forks or other pointed instruments will punch holes into the meat and let the juices out.) When you have turned the steaks, salt the uncooked side of the meat to taste and broil for about 4 minutes. When the steak is ready, the inside meat should be pink and the outside should be nicely browned. I recommend that this steak be served medium rare, so that it will be quite juicy. Cooking the meat too rare results in blood running out onto the plates when the steak is cut, and cooking it much beyond the medium rare stage starts to make the meat dry and tough. Unfortunately, however, setting cooking times to the exact second simply won't work because of variations in the thickness of the meat, the exact distance to the heat source, the intensity of the heat source, and so on. Knowing your own equipment is very important in broiling a steak—or any other meat.

For best results, put the medium rare steaks directly onto the plates and serve. The success of the dinner depends on having everything else ready, so that the steaks can be eaten immediately. With each steak serve a baked potato, a hearty green salad with some red cherry tomatoes and good French bread. Steak, for the most part, is a meat-and-potatoes dish, but I often serve up a generous helping of fresh mushrooms that have been sautéed in butter and sprinkled with a little parsley.

Remember that I use lots of pepper on these steaks. I love the smell and taste of freshly crushed pepper, and, besides, the flavor really goes with broiled beefsteak or buffalo. It might be best, however, to start off with a modest amount of pepper the first time you try this recipe. Then you can add more and more as the taste grows on you and you gain confidence. Remember also that this steak, if cooked right, is very juicy and requires no sauce of any sort. I don't even put steak sauce on the table. In fact, I don't even stock the stuff in my refrigerator, although I can quickly mix up something with Worcestershire sauce and a little catsup. I usually don't want to insult my guests, but I try to get them to at least taste the steak without sauce.

The French make a dish called *Steak au Poivre*. I think my steak is better, and is certainly much easier to prepare, but any man who is still courting, or who is so inclined, might profit from the more fancy recipe, especially on a cold, rainy night. The success of the recipe depends on having pan juices, and it is therefore cooked in a pan. I much prefer a heavy cast-iron frying pan.

Steak au Poivre

2 very good steaks
peppercorns
salt
2 tablespoons butter
½ cup beef stock (or hot water with bouillon cube)
2 ounces good brandy

2 more tablespoons butter, melted
¼ cup chopped green onions
1 clove garlic, minced

Prepare the pepper and the steaks by the directions set forth in the previous recipe. After pressing the pepper into the meat, put the steaks into the refrigerator for two hours. When you are ready to cook, melt 1 tablespoon of butter in a large frying pan. On high heat, brown the steaks on one side—about 5 minutes for 1¼-inch steaks. Turn the steaks with tongs, salt to taste, and brown the other side—about 4 minutes. Put the steaks on a heated platter.

Pour off most of the grease from the frying pan. Add 1 tablespoon butter and bring to heat. With a spatula, dislodge any bits of meat or fat that have stuck to the pan. Add chopped green onions and garlic, reduce the heat to low, and cook for 2 or 3 minutes. Turn the heat to high and stir in the beef stock. Add the brandy, reduce the heat, and simmer until the volume is reduced by half. While the sauce is simmering keep the steak warm, get everything else ready, set the table, pour the wine, and light the candles. When the sauce has thickened enough, turn off the heat and slowly stir in 2 tablespoons of melted butter.

Serve the brandy sauce over the steak. Eat with baked potato, salad, sautéed mushrooms, French bread, and hearty red wine. After dining, lead your lady to a soft rug that fronts a hearth. Build a fire and sip some brandy while the two of you, head to head, look for tandem colons in old NASA documents.

BILL PARKER'S GOAT

Bill Parker, a banker by trade, called me over to his patio one night to sample a certain sour-mash ingredient that he used in one of his favorite goat recipes. For *Field & Stream* magazine, I had written a tall tale ("Tight Lines at Taylor's") that involved a billy goat, and, while drinking and talking, I told Bill all about it, since he frequented Taylor's Barber Shop. Naturally, the subject turned to the quality of goat meat, and I related an unpleasant culinary experience with these hard-headed creatures. Here's what had happened: Beside a country road in Tennessee, near where I lived for a while, a farmer told me that he would sell me a goat for $12 if I would catch him. That wouldn't be a problem, I said, because I planned to shoot the goat and field dress it in the pasture. No, he said, that wouldn't do, as his children liked to wrestle with the goats and had grown fond of them.

Well, with the help of a friend, catching the goat wasn't as hard as I expected. The goat didn't mind wrestling with us out in the pasture, but he decided that he didn't want to get into the pick-up truck that we had borrowed. Rigged for hauling hogs, the truck had slat sides. After we finally got the goat into the thing, he tried his best to butt out the sides while we were driving to a spot in the woods suitable for slaughter. We finally got the job done—but the meat wasn't very good.

Bill listened patiently, nodding a bit, as if taking naps between sips of sour mash.

"The goat wasn't fit to eat, Bill," I said.

"Well," he said, straightening up, "The worst thing you can do with a goat is wrestle him down or chase him all over the pasture. And, regardless of what Mr. Oyette Taylor says, throwing a goat off a bridge won't help a bit. You don't want to get him mad or hot, if you're going to eat him. The best thing to do with a live goat is shoot him right between the eyes and gut him as soon as possible. Of course, you may want to—and ought to—hang the meat for a week or two in a cool place. But the real secret is to cook a goat slow." His head nodded down, as if he were about to doze off to sleep, but he jerked up again. "Real slow," he added, "and on low heat. A goat has got a lot of white fat, and you want to cook it out slowly. Never let the fat melt and drop down on hot coals. It will stink and dis- flavor the meat. That's why lots of folks don't like goat. They don't know how to cook them."

With or without sour-mash ingredients, Bill Parker has cooked more goats on his patio than any other banker of my acquaintance, so I didn't argue with him.

Shortly after that somewhat misty conversation about goats, I dropped by Bill's house one crisp morning to taste his all-night venison neck recipe, which we had discussed by telephone the previous day. Well, Bill didn't have a ven- ison neck cooked up. The neck wasn't to be found in his freezer, he said, looking me square in the eye. He said his wife had misplaced it. Then he said that his son took it. But, in any case, he had cooked up a good batch of goat, and I was fortunate enough to make away with a hind quarter.

Using a large covered charcoal grill, Bill had cooked big chunks of goat meat directly from the freezer—without even thawing them out! I had never heard of such a thing and told him so, but I can't argue with the results. So, here's Bill Parker's recipe for goat. If you don't have goat and can't get one that was properly butchered, try the rec- ipe without modification on lean pork, lamb, venison, or various cuts of beef.

Bill Parker's All-Night Goat

hind quarter of goat
½ cup cooking oil
1 cup vinegar
sour mash whiskey
4 small onions, golf-ball size
2 cloves garlic
½ small can black pepper
no salt

Before getting started, make sure you've got enough whiskey for the task at hand. Lay a medium batch of charcoal in any suitable grill unit that has a cover. While the coals get hot, take the goat meat out of the freezer. Unwrap the meat and let it stand for a few mintues, then sprinkle it heavily with black pepper. (Bill says to use half a small box, but you might want to cut back a bit.) Put the chunk of meat onto a generously large sheet of heavy-duty aluminum foil. Being careful that no sharp bones puncture the foil, form a boat shape that won't leak. Slowly pour on ½-cup of cooking oil. Then pour on the vinegar. Put the onions and the garlic on top. Pour in a little whiskey. Using the drugstore fold, seal the meat. (Having a tightly sealed package is very important, Bill says, to hold in the steam. Besides, the meat juices are needed later for gravy.) Then very carefully transfer it to the grill when the coals are hot. Close the hood. Close down the vent for slow cooking.

Ideally, the fire will burn for about 5 hours and the meat will still be warm the next morning. For maximum gastronomic delight, the meat will be almost crusted on the bottom. Before opening the foil, carefully transfer the meat to a suitable platter or shallow pan so that all the juices will be retained. Slice the meat, then serve it with the juices and onions. Good stuff.

Bill says that the vinegar used in this recipe sort of negates the need for salt. Damned if it doesn't.

For cooking a large batch of goat meat, it's hard to beat a pit in the ground. This method is ideally suited for cooking the larger pieces of meat, such as the hind quarters. It's an all-night affair, and it's great fun for a crowd of people who like an open fire. Here's my recipe:

2 goats
1 gallon prepared mustard
lots of cheesecloth
heavy-duty aluminum foil

After field dressing the goats, hang them in a meat cooler for 2 weeks. Or cut them up and put them in an ice chest for two weeks; keep the meat covered with ice, but be sure to drain out the water from time to time.

When you are ready to cook, dig a hole in the ground, about 4 feet square and 3 or 4 feet deep. Butcher the goats so that you have two hams, a saddle, and two shoulders from each. (Save the shanks, ribs, neck, and variety meats for other recipes.) Bone each goat's two shoulders and put them together, wrapping them with cotton cord, so that you have one chunk of meat. Wrap all the large pieces of meat in several layers of cheese cloth and tie it. Then souse the cloth with prepared mustard. (Mustard is cheap if you buy it by the gallon.)

At sundown, build a large fire in and over the hole. Use lots of wood, so that you will have lots of hot coals. Keep the fire going for several hours, roasting marshmallows or something, if you want to. Coat the cheese cloth again with mustard and wrap the pieces with extra heavy aluminum foil. Make sure that foil covers the bottom of each piece of meat, and seal the top and bottom pieces of foil on the sides, pointing the seam up. The idea is to keep the liquid (and steam) inside the foil and not let it drain out onto the coals.

Very carefully put the pieces of meat into the hole over the coals. The pieces of foil-covered meat can be touching, side to side, but the chunks should not be stacked. Cover the meat with dirt, and pile all the loose dirt on top. Leave the meat covered for 9 or 10 hours, or even longer. When you are ready to eat, you can cut the meat with a fork!

Warning: Before you undertake such a cookout, remember that digging a hole is sometimes difficult. In addition to hard ground or rocks, you often run into a problem with roots. Have an ax, good scoops, and plenty of help.

If you have any meat left over from either of the above recipes, you might consider the dish below. I owe this one to my good wife, who inspired it with her talk of a Kurdish shepherd who cooked something similar in a remote camp somewhere in the foothills of northern Iran. In search of an ancient village, she had been hiking in this place with friends, who, through some rather complicated family ties, knew the shepherd. The fellow had come to this place for the summer, along with a nomadic herd of sheep and goats, led, my wife said, by the oldest and ugliest nanny that you ever saw. The fellow also had a donkey, which carried such goods as an earthern pot of yogurt, a bag of oranges, and a bunch of thyme. While cooking, my wife said, the fellow kept an eye peeled for a white wolf and seemed to be quite worried about it. She thought the wolf might be a figment of some sort of local myth.

In any case, I cooked the following version with leftovers from Bill Parker's goat. If you don't have leftovers, boil some goat meat in water with a bay leaf or two until it is tender. Drain the meat, let it cool, cube it, sprinkle it with a little fresh lemon juice, and let it sit for a while. Then proceed with the following recipe:

Kurdish Shepherd's Goat

1 pound of pre-cooked goat meat, diced
1 cup goat broth, or water with bouillon cube
flour
1 medium onion, chopped
1 clove garlic
oil or butter
salt and pepper
thyme
yogurt
rice, cooked separately (see next chapter)

Heat some oil or goat butter in a large frying pan with a lid. Sauté the onion and garlic for a few minutes. Add the diced meat, sprinkle with flour, and stir. Turn to high heat. Add the broth. Bring to boil, stir in salt and pepper to taste, reduce heat, and simmer without covering until the liquid is reduced by half. Serve the goat and gravy over precooked rice, topped with yogurt and garnished with fresh thyme, which is eaten raw along with the goat, rice, and yogurt. If you don't have fresh thyme, or don't care for it, try a sprig or two of fresh parsley, carrot tops, or some such dainty greens.

Enjoy this dish on the patio or on the heath—but beware the white eidolon.

TO HELL WITH THE TEXAS RIG

"But it's not really barbecue," the hefty red-bearded guy said, scooping up another forkful. On his third helping now, he wasn't exactly timid about eating my dish, whatever he thought it was.

A number of possible replies popped to mind, but I didn't like to use strong language in mixed company. In any case, my wife headed me off, asking very politely whether anyone wanted another glass of iced tea.

Nobody wanted any tea.

"I'll take a little more of this stuff," the guy said, reaching for the platter of barbecue. He sported a Hawaiian shirt and shorts, and, as I sized him up, I realized that he had expected a patio dinner when we invited him and his wife over for barbecued venison. He didn't look like a Texan and I doubted that he was connected with that gang from San Antonio that had been after me for 11 years. On this Texas matter, I'm guilty only of speaking the plain truth in the wrong place. But I said it then and I say it now: there are better ways to rig a plastic worm—and venison barbecued over open fire or coals is too dry, no matter how much gook is swabbed on it. But it's not my fault that Alaska, not Texas, is now the nation's largest state, or that the world's best recipe for barbecued venison is of Alaskan origin, not Texan.

"What I meant," he said, "is that real barbecue is cooked outside. Over wood or charcoal."

This time the guy's wife tried to changed the subject, turning to shop talk about education. Both women taught high school.

"I don't care what you say," I said, looking the man in

the eye. "If it looks like barbecue and smells like barbecue and tastes like barbecue——"

"Drop it, A.D.," my wife said, almost in a whisper. I don't know what she was so worried about. The fist fight that I had 16 years ago on the end of a public fishing pier in Florida was about Apalachacola oysters. It had nothing whatsoever to do with barbecue. All I said to that bearded fellow from Baltimore was that the best oysters from Apalachacola came in late September after a dry spell, at which time and condition the water in the bay was low and had the right salinity to produce small, lean, manageable oysters with great flavor. I suppose he took these facts as being an affront on the big, fat mollusks of Chesapeake Bay.

"Oh, it's good," the guy said. "I'll allow that it's as good as barbecue. In fact, I sure would like to have the recipe for this sauce." That said, he shovelled another forkful into the hole in his beard.

"It's not just the sauce," I said. "Look, you can't isolate the sauce from the dish and then smear it on venison that some jackleg has dried out over coals." Seeing that my wife was getting fidgety again, I decided to smooth the argument over with a joke. "As an old timer here in town once told me—"

"That's not very appropriate," my wife said.

"I'd love to hear it," the woman said, nervously.

"This old timer said that folks used to eat in the house and go to the bathroom out in the yard. Now, by gum, he says, they go to the bathroom in the house and eat out in the yard."

The laughter wasn't quite as loud as I had expected, and I decided not to follow up with my pitch about patio cookery being a conspiracy of women's-lib organizations and promoted by feminist magazines.

The guy seemed to consider the old joke seriously. "Well," he said, licking his lips after having polished up his plate, "If you're going to cook barbecue——"

"Stop it! Both of you!" my wife said, stamping her foot | *30* like a school teacher. "Now let's look at this matter logically. A.D.'s recipe originated in Alaska. Right? Oh, to be sure, he *perfected* the dish, but it *is* of Alaskan origin, right?"

Right.

"Well, it was developed by necessity," she continued. "Why? Obviously because it's often too cold in Alaska to cook outside all the time. It's as simple as that and we don't need to discuss it further."

"I'm not a frigging Eskimo," the guy said, licking his lips, "but I'll certainly buy that argument."

Well, that seemed to settle the matter and I decided to change the subject, asking, "What part of Texas did you say you folks are from?"

"You already asked that," my wife said.

"We're from Upper Michigan," his wife said, "and we sure would like to have a copy of your delicious indoor barbecue recipe to send back home, where it's often too cold to cook outside." She stood up, as if the party were over and the matter settled. "Now if you two fellows will work on the recipe, I'll help do the dishes." From her purse she removed a yellow pencil and handed it to me.

Well, there wasn't anything to do but start writing. Here's what I put down on a paper towel for the gastronomical benefit of the good people of Upper Michigan:

A.D.'s Stove-top Dutch Oven Barbecue

2 pounds venison, boneless
½ pound bacon
1 cup chopped onions
2 cloves of garlic, minced

1 cup catsup

½ cup of red wine vinegar

¼ cup of Worcestershire sauce

¼ cup of brown sugar

salt and pepper

rice, cooked separately

Cut venison into pieces no larger than 1-inch cubes. In the bottom of a dutch oven (or large frying pan) cook bacon over a gas or electric stove eye until it is crisp. Remove bacon, crumble, and set aside. In a bowl or other container, mix all ingredients except venison and rice. (Salt and pepper to taste, or try 1 tablespoon of salt and ⅛ teaspoon of pepper.) Drain venison and brown it in bacon drippings. Pour off drippings and liquid. Add other ingredients except rice. Stir well. Cover tightly and simmer for about an hour, or until meat is tender. Stir occasionally. Cook rice.

Serve barbecued venison on rice. Feeds seven or eight ordinary people.

What I didn't tell them, but should have, is that the rice is an important part of the dish. Use only long grain rice. Short rice tends to stick together, and the only time I want gooky rice is when I'm eating, or trying to eat, with chopsticks. Even long grain rice, however, will stick if it isn't prepared right. My good wife is the resident rice expert, and here's how she cooks it:

Helen's Rice

4 cups water

2 cups rice

salt to taste

Bring salted water to boil. Add rice and turn heat down to low. Cover with lid. (The boiler must be tightly covered.) Cook exactly 20 minutes over low heat. Prepare another pan of cold water. Remove rice boiler from heat and place it into the pan of cold water. (Water should cover about half the depth of the boiler.) Return boiler to warm stove eye. Let sit for two or three minutes. Then remove the lid and serve at once.

It's important—or mandatory around our house—that the lid not be removed from the boiler, not even to take a peek, until the end of the procedure. I won't say that my wife is fussy, but on this matter she is of firm opinion. All rice, she says, should be prepared in this manner, except for that used in *lubyah peleau,* which is an old Persian recipe that she learned to cook when she taught school in Iran shortly before the revolution. She can also pronounce the name of this dish, which sounds very sophisticated—until you come to the meat of it.

Getting back to Alaskan barbecue, I might add that, in addition to cooking the rice properly and not looking at it for 20 minutes, some prior attention to the meat may be in order. Such cuts as the tenderloin can be used as is, but tough meat should be marinated over night. Every great chef has favorite marinades and I'm no exception. The best one I've found is ordinary milk. Simply put the meat in a suitable container, cover it with milk, and refrigerate for 15 hours or so. This method of tenderizing wild game was used by the settlers when they pushed westward and didn't always have all manner of spice and such. It works just as well today as it did back then, and I prefer it because it doesn't disflavor the meat.

Marinade aside, the basic recipe given above has become our all-time favorite way of preparing venison. Moreover, it can also be used for other game, domestic meat, and fowl. It smells good. It tastes good. It even has a deep, rich color. Why, this recipe would make downright delectable eating from even an old scrawny Texas longhorn cow. Or, for that

matter, from an Upper Michigan moose of either sex. I
don't think the recipe would help fat Chesapeake Bay
oysters, but I'm a sporting man and I'll lay even money that
it will beat _lubyah peleau_ any day for cooking up tough old
Iranian mountain goats. And whether or not it should be
called barbecue would not be questioned by anyone. Except
maybe the Texicans.

The aforementioned San Antonio gang and the Texas
worm rig might require futher explanation. Some years
back, I wrote an article called "To Hell with the Texas
Rig," and from that good state I received some very bad
letters. But I said it then and I stand by it now: day in and
day out, you'll catch more fish with a plastic worm threaded
onto a weedless hook instead of rigging the thing Texas
style, with the hook's point hidden in the body of the plastic. Yes, it's true that the bass will _take_ Texas-rigged worms
readily, and, yes, it's true that the rig is indeed weedless
enough to drag through a patch of submerged mesquite
bushes. But the rig simply doesn't hook fish efficiently.

Because of the Texas rig, the fishing rods of the 1970's
were too stiff and the lines were too heavy, and anglers fell
out of boats or broke off the pedestal of their seats trying to
set the hook. Worms became softer and softer, and Tom
Mann, touting the Jelly worm, grew rich. Then, while the
worms got softer and softer, the manufacturers started the
search for a better worm hook. Just look at a current bass-
tackle catalog and you'll see Messler rotating hooks, Tru-
Turn hooks, Speed Sticker hooks, Colt 45, and who knows
what else. Indeed the search for a better worm hook ought
to be ample evidence that something was fundamentally
amiss from the start. But after a certain point of no return
too many of the bass pros had sold their names and pictures
to go on advertisements, and had been on too many TV
shows, and in too many articles, to suddenly call the Texas
rig what it was.

Still, I beseech them—the bass pros, the worm manufactures, Ray Scott, outdoor writers, George Bush, *somebody*—to do *something*. We are simply feeding our bass and snapping turtles too much soft plastic.

But manufacturers, bass pros, Texicans, magazine writers, and TV shows aren't likely to change. Soft worms sell by the untold millions, simply because the angler has to take a sackful of them out fishing. What I'm looking for, however, is a hard plastic worm, a worm that will stay on a weedless hook for half a day without re-rigging, a worm that feels natural, a worm that bass like to mouth and won't spit out. (Yes, the bass are spitting out the worms. Why else would manufacturers now be touting worms with various additives or attachments, such as velcro collars, to cause the worm to become entangled in the bass's fine teeth, thereby causing the lure to stay in the fish's mouth long enough for the angler to set the hook?) Yes, I say again, yes, bass spit out ultrasoft plastic worms. What would you do if you bit down on what looked like an eel or other good meat, but felt something softly strange, like jello? You'd spit it out and look at it, no matter whether you be in New Hampshire, North Carolina, Southern California, or Texas.

It's the same with venison. What would you do if you sat down at a board to eat what you thought would be succulent venison and bit down on a big mouthful of hard meat that had been soused in barbecue sauce? You'd spit it out to see what it was. That's what I did—and that's what made the San Antonio boys mad. To hell with 'em.

GREG RANE'S BOSTON BUTT— AND KATHLEEN'S COMPLAINT

Not a cloud floated in the big sky above Compass Lake. Not a puff of wind rippled the waters. Before setting out, however, Old Man Oscar Roney, as Daddy and the Judge called him, looked to the North, to the South, to the East, and to the West, sniffing the air like a fox. Finally, we left the womenfolks at the cabin and started rowing and paddling the small boat toward a stand of cypress trees near the distant shore. We seemed to zigzag our way, and it soon became clear to me that we would get to our fishing hole faster, and with half as much work, if the men would coordinate their strokes. The Judge wanted to know where in the world I picked up a big word like "coordinate," so I didn't say any more about it. But Mr. Oscar kind of winked at me, as if he thought I might have a point.

We were after shellcracker bream and softshelled turtles. The Judge was especially eager to get hold of another softshell, for eating purposes. Mr. Oscar had already fried a 30-pounder for us in a cast-iron washpot that sat over scrub oak coals. The turtle meat tasted mighty good, just like Mr. Oscar said it would, and even the womenfolks enjoyed it.

Mr. Oscar knew not only how to catch, dress, and cook softshelled turtles but also how to beat them at their own game. Turning a softshell over on its back in the bottom of a boat, for example, didn't mean anything whatsoever, unless you first cut off its head and that arm-long neck, with which it could flip right over. The trick, of course, is to get the turtle to stick out his head and then cut it off without getting bit or swamping the boat. Mr. Oscar knew also that the gopher tortoise, which at that time lived so abundantly in the sandhills of this part of Florida, were just as good or even better than softshells for eating purposes.

Mr. Oscar knew something about everything, and he had even built the little cypress boat that we were fishing from. Mr. Oscar knew that the small freshwater shrimp here in Compass Lake made good bait for bluegills. Mr. Oscar knew that the warmouth perch lived in the cypress stumps, as well as in hollow logs, and could be caught with top water minnows on a #4 hook. Mr. Oscar knew that shell-crackers bedded on sand bottom in the deeper waters away from the stand of cypress trees and were best caught on earthworms. Mr. Oscar knew that the green trout (which is what we called largemouth bass) lived in the lily pad cove just beyond the cypress stand.

Indeed, Mr. Oscar's knowledge of fishing lore seemed endless, and some of his ideas, it seemed to me, were highly practical. For example, when we approached our fishing hole he quit rowing and drifted in, then told Daddy to ease the anchor down instead of throwing it in with a splash. An annoying thing about Mr. Oscar, however, was that he measured things mostly in "mites" and spoke mostly in simple sentences without explanation. Being young and inexperienced, of course, I wanted to know the why of things in some detail.

After a while, however, Daddy told me to refrain from asking Mr. Oscar any more questions.

"Why?" I asked.

Daddy told me to shut my mouth and not open it again for any reason whatsoever. And be still. Quit rocking the boat. Stay out of Mr. Oscar's fishing sack. Quit scratching redbugs (which is what we called chiggers). I had noticed that Mr. Oscar, slightly stooped as he watched his float, was indeed getting a little nervous even before we got to fishing good, and I figured that maybe I had "Mr. Oscared" him a mite too much. But I wanted to shout out that I wouldn't have asked Mr. Oscar so many dadburned questions in the first place if I had been allowed to fish.

Perhaps I had better explain that one. Our boat had been designed for only two people, and there had been some heated discussion back at the cabin about whether or not I could come along with the men. Daddy's argument was that the boat simply wasn't large enough for four people, all with long fishing poles. I knew that Daddy had a point— but I also knew that Mama had a way of getting around points. She made a case of her own, saying, "Gordon Livingston, you don't *have* to take along a washtub full of beer." Then, shaking a finger at the Judge, she added, "And don't you say a word about that, Willard Mitchell!"

In the end, Mr. Oscar suggested that I be allowed to go along, but that we take only three poles. I could help him fish, Mr. Oscar said, and could in fact have his pole after they caught a good mess of shellcrackers or turtle, whichever came first. So, I had to watch for a while, and I guess I watched too closely—and asked too many questions.

Sitting tight-lipped in the bow of the boat, pouting a little after having been told to shut up, I put my legs around the cool tub of iced-down beer, which seemed to ease the redbug problem, and watched the puffs of fast-moving clouds that had started to come our way. Before long, the bottle opener slipped out of Daddy's hand and bounced overboard. (This was before the day of easy-off bottle caps.) I saved the day with a notched blade of my Boy Scout knife, and soon I was opening a bottle of beer on a pretty regular basis for Daddy, and even more frequently for the Judge, who could turn up a bottle and drink off half of it, his adam's apple just a-pumping. Mr. Oscar also took a beer from time to time, but not many.

We were anchored a mite out from the cypress stand when the first black cloud bellowed out from the south. To the north another thunderhead gathered, and Mr. Oscar said that maybe we had better head on in 'cause he figured the clouds were going to meet up right over Compass Lake. If they did, he said, it would be hell to pay. Daddy and the Judge didn't like the idea of having to paddle back across the lake so soon, without a single fish or turtle for the womenfolks, but Mr. Oscar said he could feel a mite of electricity in the air. It made the hair on his head tingle, he said, notwithstanding the fact that both he and the Judge were as bald as hickory nuts. Suddenly a bolt of lightning struck to the south. After that, neither Daddy nor the Judge argued any further and seemed eager to get started.

Heading the bow of the boat straight across the lake, Mr. Oscar manned the oars from the middle seat while Daddy and the Judge, sitting side by side, each wielded a paddle from the stern seat. The waves got choppy, and we didn't make much progress. Mr. Oscar kept looking first at the black cloud looming up from the south and then at the darkening turbulence bearing down upon us from the north. From time to time he would look across the lake to see how much further we had to go. Then he would frown and shake his head, as if puzzled. Judging by the distance to the cypress trees near our fishing spot, I knew that we were not making much headway, if any. Half a mile or so off, lightning popped a tall pine tree atop one of the sandhills.

"Damn!" Mr. Oscar said. "Let's speed her up, boys. Heave ho!"

"Damn!" said the Judge, "That lightening scared the pee out of me. If I hadn't been drinking beer I'd be wet as water!"

They all laughed, albeit uneasily.

"Judge," Daddy said, chuckling, "I thought you relieved yourself a while ago."

(Only by way of explanation do I add that Mr. Oscar didn't allow anyone to stand up in his small boat, and all calls of nature had to be answered from a kneeling or a squatting position, depending, Mr. Oscar said, on what you had to do and what you had to do it with. We had a 1-gallon syrup bucket aboard for that purpose.)

"I wasn't a-peeing, Gordon," the Judge said. "I was a-praying." They all got to laughing again, and the Judge added, "And I hope that it's only a fart that you or Oscar have let loose."

They quit laughing when suddenly lightning struck closer, sparking around in a tight clump of tall cypress trees on the bank, as if the Lord Himself had thrown a bolt at us for cussing and drinking beer and farting. This speeded things up considerably. Both the Judge and Daddy paddled so furiously for a while that they slung water all the way to the bow of the boat, wetting me good. Mr. Oscar wasn't going fast, but I could tell that (1) he was taking bigger bites with the oars, and that (2) he was straining much harder, bending the oars to the cracking point, it seemed. He began to sweat. In spite of the increased labor, however, the old cypress boat didn't move much, even though it seemed to be kind of bucking in the water, as if raring to go but couldn't. The waves kept coming harder and higher, some breaking over the bow. Daddy said it was twister weather.

"Son," Mr. Oscar said, "Rinse the pee out of that syrup bucket. Flatten the mouth a mite, making a scoop, just in case we have to bail her out." He always referred to his little boat in the feminine gender.

I did it.

"Can you bail water, son?" Mr. Oscar asked, seriously now.

"Yes, sir, I sure can," I said, scooping up a little, "but . . . maybe there's something else that we ought to do, too." I glanced at Daddy.

"What's that, Son?" Daddy asked, nicely now, maybe thinking that he had been too hard on me and maybe he ┃ *40* had played hell by letting Mama talk him into bringing such a young boy into such dangerous waters on such a small boat in the first place. "Go on and say it, Son."

"I think she would go faster if you would pull up the anchor," I said.

"Hot-a'mighty-damn!" Mr. Oscar said, reaching down by the side of the boat for the white anchor rope that cut through the clear waters. "That's what's holding her, boys!"

Weighing anchor speeded the boat up considerably. We all got back to the other side of Compass Lake safe and sound, and only partly wet, dodging lightning bolts as we came. After we had determined that the womenfolks were all right, the Judge put his hand on my head, saying, "Ay God, Gordon, I think this boy could coordinate paddling much better if you would let him speak a little more frequently!"

A quarter of a century later, give or take a year or two, a young lady with various talents caught my eye. But, alas, she had been brainwashed into thinking that she liked to ski on water. To gain first hand knowledge of how serious this condition was, I agreed to go with her to a family gathering down on Compass Lake. She had two brothers, both married with kids of their own, all ski-whizzes and hamburger freaks. These people, and others like them, streaked across the waters of the main part of Compass Lake in such numbers that serious fishing was pretty much out of the question.

The stand of cypress trees had gotten smaller—or I had gotten bigger—since I first fished here with Daddy, Judge Mitchell, and Old Man Oscar Roney. One large cove, however, over beyond the clump of cypress trees, looked very, very good to me, and of course I started thinking bass. Cypress Trout, Old Man Oscar had called them. The cove had thick grass along the banks. Large patches of lily pads grew here and there. Quite a few cypress trees and stumps stuck up. Perfect. When I commented that the cove was pretty, the whole family looked at me most strangely. I think they were trying to get some sort of legal injunction permitting their boat club to clean the cypress stumps out of the cove so that it would be suitable for water skiing. "Pretty," to them, was open water. Wide open.

Anyhow, one of their neighbors had a 14-foot aluminum john boat. I borrowed it, figuring that I could paddle the young lady around in the cove and show her how to catch some bass, especially late in the afternoon, thereby modifying her notions of how to spend a perfect weekend. In a corner of the cabin I found an old pushbutton rod and reel combo with a little line on it, along with a few plastic worms (black with white spots) and weedless worm hooks. Of course, I would have preferred to have my bait-casting outfit, but, on the other hand, my future fishing partner had never made a cast in her life. I had, in fact, planned to let her do all of the fishing, if she could, and I knew that the pushbutton reel would be easier for her to use. Further, I was here primarily to court the young lady, not to untangle birdsnests made by backlashes.

"OK," I said, after pushing away from the dock and expertly paddling the johnboat to within casting range of a patch of lily pads, "Cast the worm next to the pads, let it sink down until your line goes slack, then start your retrieve, working the rod tip slightly——"

Swish went the rod. Up with the worm. It came down about half way between the boat and the lily pads.

"OK," I said, patiently. "Now let the worm sink—no, no, don't reel it in so fast. Look, a worm is *not* a crankbait. You've got to give it a little action. Stop and go, stop and go." With my hands I twitched an imaginary worm along, and I had to check my instinct to reach for the rod.

She cranked in the worm steadily until it was about a foot from the rod tip. Then she drew back and let it fly again. Again the worm went almost straight up.

"You need to cast a little lower, honey," I said, pushing some air down with the palm of my hand.

"Why?" she asked.

"Because in some spots you will have to cast under trees and overhanging brush or even up under boat docks."

"But there are no trees or brush or boat docks out here," she said, reeling in the worm straight and steady. Then she threw it up and away again.

"All right," I said. "I'll paddle the boat in closer so that when you cast it up, it will at least land nearer the line of pads."

On the next cast, the worm shot out like a bullet, landing 20 yards or better inside the pads. She let it sink. On the retrieve, of course, the worm caught in the crotch of the largest, strongest lily pad in Florida. She couldn't snatch it loose. I took the rod, but I couldn't finesse the hook loose and I was reluctant to apply brute force. I suspected that the line wasn't too good, being old and frayed. Because we had a limited supply of lures, I decided to paddle into the pads to get the worm.

"Please," I said, after retrieving the spotted worm, rerigging it, and patiently maneuvering the boat into position again. "Please don't cast so far back into the lily pads." She had no experience and I didn't know what she would do with a bass if she hooked into one back in there. The boat was, I admit, a little unwieldy.

"You just told me *not* to throw it up but to throw it straight," she said. "If I throw it straight——"

"OK. You were . . . I was just worried about you getting hung up again, that's all," I said. "However you want to fish is all right with me. I'll just paddle us out a little so you can——"

"Fine," she said, turning in her seat and casting the worm far out into the open water. She seemed a little irritated at me.

43 | "The bass will be a mite nearer the lily pads," I said.

"But you just told me that I would get hung up in the damned lily pads," she said, stamping her feet up and down, scaring the bass.

"All right. Whatever," I said. "No, no, don't just reel it in like that. Let it sink. You've got to let it sink, especially out in that deeper water."

"I think something's got it," she said, somewhat matter-of-factly, lowering her rod tip to give slack. She seemed concerned that she would hurt whatever was on the other end.

"Snatch it! Snatch it!" I yelled, standing, as the line cut the water, arcing off the port side of the bow.

"You just told me to let it sink!"

"Reel in the goddamn slack and set the hook!" I advised.

She started reeling. "Something's got it again!" she said when she hit the end of the slack line.

"Snatch it," I shouted.

The rod bent. She cranked and pointed the rod straight away as the reel's drag sang.

"Hold up the rod," I said, helping her with it. "Oh no! Don't crank against the drag! You'll twist your line. You need to set the hook."

"Do you want me to pull in this thing or not?" she asked, stopping and looking at me.

"Yes. No. Yes. Listen. Keep a tight line while your drag is working. When the drag quits slipping, pump the fish in with the rod, then reel in the slack when you lower the rod. I'm not sure you've even stuck the fish. Maybe you ought to set the hook now." I reached over and gave the rod a jerk for her, trying to stick the hook.

She gave me a dirty look and started cranking on the reel handle again. The fish swirled at the boat and made another drag-stripping run toward open water. Three pounds. Maybe three and a half. It turned. It jumped, it's red gills flashing.

"Jesus, we need a net," I said. "Ease it up to the boat and I'll try to lip it for you. Don't horse it now."

She reeled the line in until the rod tip was almost in the bass's mouth. Then she snatched the fish out of the water. The line broke just as the bass cleared the side of the johnboat. It came down inside the gunnel and started flopping around on the aluminum deck.

"Damn!" I said. "We don't even have a stringer."

"What kind of fish is it?" she asked.

"Bass. Largemouth. I'll keep my foot on it until it quits flopping." Holding the fish down, I quickly rerigged the worm for her and paddled in toward the pads again.

"It's looking at me," she said.

I turned the fish around, saying, "OK, just relax now and cast the worm up next to those pads. See that large cypress stump just under the water? Cast just to the right of it. Let it sink about——"

Swish. Out went the worm again—out, out, and into open water.

"Honey, honey . . . ."

"I think something's got it again," she said almost as soon as it splashed down. It seemed that a bass had been waiting for that spotted plastic worm.

"You really ought to set the hook," I said.

She reeled in slowly while the fish zinged her drag. The bass jumped quickly, as if puzzled about this bizarre method of fishing. And this bass was big enough to know a little something about fishing. I guessed its weight to be at around 7 pounds. (Later, one of her ski-whiz brothers said it was big enough to stuff and hang on the wall of the cabin. He's the same one who asked me how many *I* had caught. This jerk couldn't even cook a hamburger, much less catch a green trout.) How she got the thing into the boat I'll never know. Nor do I know exactly what I did to help her. I do know that, after the battle had been won, she wasn't in much of a mood to talk, and the poor girl must have been utterly exhausted. She told me, in short, to just keep the damned rod.

Those small bass seemed to be hitting very well in the open water, and I thought that surely anyone with casting skill could catch a real lunker back in the lily pads. Fourteen pounds? Why not! So, since the young lady was already tired of fishing, I kept the rod and handed her the paddle. For an hour or so, I cast perfectly to the line of pads whenever the boat got in close enough. The problem, of course, was that she couldn't keep the boat in position. She couldn't even keep it pointed in the right direction. Instead of proceeding on toward what appeared to be a feeder creek hotspot at the end of the cove, she kept heading, albeit on a zigzag course, back toward the cabin. I soon concluded that the young lady didn't know any more about paddling a boat than she did about bass fishing.

In any case, the fact that I wasn't about to straddle a set of water skis, along with the young lady's reluctance to gain further experience in the art of boat paddling, did nothing to strengthen our relationship. But, as any bassman will confirm, I had given this young lady some very good bass fishing advice. What she choose to do with it would be her business—and soon was.

A quarter of a century later, give or take a year or two, I again found myself on Compass Lake. For this trip my good wife and I had joined Greg and Kathleen Rane at their cottage, along with a bunch of kids, both ours and theirs. (I won't have much to say about the kids, lest this chapter go on far too long, but I'll note here that I doubt whether there was a dozen redbugs on the whole lot of 'em.) Frankly, I had come here for food and fellowship and a drink or two, not for bass fishing. In fact, I hadn't even brought along my fishing gear. Both family cars had been pretty well packed, and, a wiser man since I gave my wife that boat battery for our anniversary, I recognized the trip as being hazardous to graphite and boron baitcasting rods, not to mention flyrods, flipping rods, and spinning rods. Besides, Rane had said that he had plenty of fishing gear. Pushbutton stuff and cane poles.

Another reason for not fishing was that I knew in my heart that Compass Lake had become even more of a water skier's haven during the past 25 years. I was right. The cypress stand had gotten even smaller, it seemed, but the cove was still pretty much as I remembered it from the previous trip, except that the shoreline contained more cabins. But cabins were much better than the high rise apartments that I had fully expected.

With the aid of Rane's cane poles, I set out to catch us a softshell or two off the dock. I had wanted a 30-pound turtle so that we could get a 7- or 8-pound roast from the hind part for eating purposes. Rane fancied himself to be an accomplished patio chef, and I wanted to see what he could do with some really good meat. But I failed to catch a softshell. Maybe they had gone the way of the gopher tortoise, now a protected species even in the sandhills of North Florida.

On over toward sundown, however, my wife put in to go bass fishing. I also had the urge to go, but I restrained myself and stayed off the water, having learned long ago that serious bass fishing in mixed company simply doesn't work. My wife settled for making a few casts off the dock with Rane's pushbutton gear. I had a turtle pole sticking out on either side of the dock, so I told her that for bass she ought to cast straight out into open water. Seeing that a buzz bait was tied onto her line, I advised her to cast high.

"The buzz bait will flutter down like a wounded bird," I explained, "attracting bass as it comes. When it hits the water, retrieve it as fast as you can crank, so that the bass will think it is trying to get away."

On her first cast, a 5-pounder nailed the buzz bait. Immediately it started jumping and shaking its head with enough show to draw everybody out of the cabin and onto the dock. After helping my wife set the hook, I finally got the bass up to the dock for her without much trouble. It really wasn't my fault that she didn't know how to lip the bass properly and thereby lost a little skin off her thumb when it flounced back into Compass Lake.

Rane quickly came to the rescue with a first aid kit. After pouring some Mercurochrome onto my wife's thumb, he went to work with bandage gauze, saying, "I'll tell you, that A.D. knows more about bass fishing than anyone I've ever known. The so-called experts around here tell me to fish in the weeds—where you get all tangled up. How ridiculous! Yes sir, A.D. knows exactly how to catch bass."

"I've written four books on bass fishing," I said, watching my turtle sets.

"*I* caught the fish," my wife said, pointing the bandged thumb toward herself. It was red on the end.

"Yeah, but A.D. told you exactly what to do," Rane said, sipping on his beer. My wife didn't answer. Kathleen didn't say anything either, but she lowered her sunglasses and looked at Rane. "Yeah, well, OK," he said, glancing at the sun, which was getting low on the horizon now. "I guess I had better go build the fire."

"I'll help you," I said, knowing that no self respecting softshell was going to bite while the kids were stomping around the dock and women were slinging buzz baits into the water.

On the patio, Rane immediately started making excuses, saying that his little cabin grill didn't cook as good as his big 940 back home. I also pointed out to him, right off, that he had forgotten to bring along his meat thermometer. He looked at me questioningly.

"Never cook a thick piece of meat, especially pork," I explained, pulling up a patio chair, "unless you've got a meat thermometer. That way, you'll know when it's done— but not too done."

"Is that a fact?" Rane said, twisting the cap off another | *48* bottle of beer. Then he proceeded to cook the Boston butt, a little nervously at first. But a beer or two settled him down and he shared with me the secrets of the grill as well as the rewards. The man obviously enjoyed what he was doing. In the same spirit I pass on the following preparatory details on what turned out to be a memorable piece of meat.

Greg Rane's Boston Butt

Several hours before cooking, put some hickory chunks in water for soaking. Then, when you are ready to cook, lay a charcoal fire in one end of a large grill that has a cover or hood for smoking. (Putting the coals on one end of the grill is important because the meat will go on the opposite side. This method works best with a rather large grill.) Rane says that building a good charcoal fire is part of the cooking, and he won't have truck with the newfangled gas heated lava rock grills. Further, he says, those "smoker/cooker" units simply won't work for this recipe.

To start a fire, he says, lay your coals in a pile on one side of the grill. Light the fire. Let the charcoal burn down for about 30 minutes. While waiting, check off your list of stuff to make sure you've got everything you need:

fresh Boston butt, 4 to 6 pounds

two sticks butter

1 cup white vinegar

6 tablespoons fresh lemon juice

3 tablespoons garlic powder

black pepper

bottle of lemon-pepper seasoning salt

Bone the Boston butt (a common cut of meat from a pork shoulder) and let the meat warm to room temperature. To mix a basting sauce, melt the butter and stir in the lemon juice, garlic powder, white vinegar, and black pepper to taste. (Rane goes heavy on the pepper, heisting his left leg a little as he sprinkles it on.) Be sure to use garlic powder, not garlic salt. The basting sauce should be kept hot throughout the cooking process, Rane maintains.

When the fire is right, place the Boston butt fat side down on the grill opposite from the pile of coals. To the coals add four or five chunks of soaked hickory wood. Close the hood.

After 15 minutes, open the hood and baste the Boston butt. After basting, sprinkle the meat generously with lemon pepper. Repeat this process every 15 minutes, making sure to sprinkle on the lemon pepper *after* basting the meat. Also, make sure that you close the hood after each basting. Never turn the meat. Never use salt.

Cook the Boston butt for 2 or 3 hours, depending on how hot the fire is. Rane says that a cool fire allows longer cooking, giving the chef the opportunity to enjoy good company and a favorite beverage. To that end, he recommends 225 to 250 degrees.

"After the meat is done," Rane says, "take it up and place it in a pan. Let it sit for about 15 minutes. Slice and serve. Any basting sauce that is left can be poured over this delicious dish."

"Well, Rane," I said, slicing off some more Boston butt at the dinner table later that night, "I would advise you to get yourself a good meat thermometer and learn how to use it if you're going to cook big chunks of meat like this." I chewed on some of the new helping. This slice had been taken further from the end, and it was even more succulent than my first helping. "Those little scrub oak trees that grow down here would be better for smoking than the hickory chips you were using. Use 'em green. Wouldn't have to soak 'em. That's what Old Man Oscar Roney used to use," I pointed out. "Also, you might find some sassafras roots in the ditches along the roadway. And I noticed that you've got a wild pecan tree in the corner of your lot. Green pecan wood works wonders on goat. Doesn't it, Sassafras?"

Ignoring my term of endearment, my wife frowned at me a little and shook her head, apparently wanting to keep the conversation off goat meat and such. Whatever bothered her (not counting my previous experience on Compass Lake) had started back at breakfast. I had said something about chicken eggs and one of the kids left the table.

"Of course, that hickory wood is hard to beat for flavoring hog meat," I added, slicing off another helping or two. "Smells good, too. I'll tell you, Rane, if you'll work on this recipe a little bit more, you may find yourself in my next book."

"And that," Kathleen said, almost as though she had been waiting for an opening, "brings up the 'Chauvinistic Chefs' sidebar in that other book that you wrote, Livingston."

"How's that?" I asked, acting as though I was somewhat puzzled.

"You've got Greg doing this and you've got A.D. doing that, and there's not a word about Helen and Kathleen, except as 'our women.' Your women indeed! It *is* chauvinistic. From cover to cover."

"Oh, Kathleen," Rane said, smiling. "A.D. is just telling it like it is."

A silence followed. Even the kids felt it, but none of them was allowed to speak just now.

"Exactly how 'is it,' Greg?" Kathleen asked.

Another silence.

"It's just a book, Kathleen," I said.

"I'm waiting for an answer," she said, staring at Rane.

"Well, a woman's place is definitely *not* on the patio, honey," he said, trying to make a joke of it. "Now, will you please jump up and run get me another cold beer," he said, adding another joke to the first one, intending no insult to injury.

"Jump up and run get your own damn beer, Sassafras," she said, in no uncertain tone.

"Kathleen," I quickly said, grabbing the salad bowl, "This lettuce and stuff that you and Helen tossed up for us makes about the best salad I've ever tasted anywhere. Bar none. I'll swear it beseems publication. Er, will you pass me a little of that meat to go with it? And please, Kathleen, *please* don't tell me to jump up and get my own Boston butt!"

The children started giggling, as I knew they would, and soon all the company was again in good cheer. Except for my wife, who was still fretting about that little ol' bass that got back into Compass Lake and complaining about her bandaged thumb.

"Did I ever tell you about the first time I came to Compass Lake some years ago?" I asked, leaning back to enjoy the company, wishing that I had a cigar, although I had quit smoking. "That little clump of cypress trees over yonder——"

"I'm going to fish off the dock a while," my son said, pushing back his chair. "Where's that buzz bait?"

"I'm watching TV," another child said, apparently speaking for the rest of the siblings as well. They all jumped up and raced for the best seats.

"I'm doing the dishes," Kathleen said.

"I'm helping Kathleen," my wife said.

"I'm getting a beer," Rane said, grunting a little as he stood. "Can I bring you one, A.D.?"

Whether or not anyone wants to know about it, I'm here to say that the cypress trees in Compass Lake have stood up pretty well for half a century. What the future holds remains to be seen. In any case, I shall be more than happy to give a quarterly update or two, in some detail, during Century 21.

DEALING WITH DUCK

The best English teacher that I've ever known taught in a high school near a tourist trap in the south of Florida. She was especially fond of the seafood in some of the local restaurants, and her son, aged 10 at the time, also loved seafood. Always he wanted to order stone crabs when they went out to eat. He seldom got them. Stone crabs were in very, very short supply at that time. (Back then the fishermen kept the whole crab; now, they pull off one claw, which must be of legal size, and the stone crab grows another.) In short, the price of stone crab was rather beyond the range of a school teacher's salary, especially since she ask for and received no alimony from her former husband.

Once a suitor in the investment business invited them out to eat at a relatively swanky tourist place down on the beach—the most expensive restaurant in the area. The guy wasn't what you would call rich, but of course he enjoyed a good salary, had investments of his own, and could afford stone crab. That's exactly what the boy ordered. The English teacher shook her head and pursed her lips, indicating a firm "no." The stone crabs, of course, cost a good deal more than steak, and, in this restaurant, they were exceeded in price only by a whole roasted Long Island duck, which was served up on a large platter with all sorts of stuffings and trimmings.

Sensing a deadlock, the waitress turned to the banker and took his order for fried shrimp. The teacher ordered boiled shrimp for herself. Squirming a little under the waitress's gaze and impatient yellow pencil, the boy said, "Can't I, Mom, please?"

"No," she said.

"Why?"

"You *know* why. We have already discussed this, young man."

"Mom-m-m."

"Stone crab is *too* expensive," she said. "Get blue crab."

"I don't want old picky blue crab."

"O.K. Get Alaskan king crab."

"I don't want ol' stringy legs," he said.

The teacher slapped her menu shut and looked at the waitress, saying, "Just bring him an order of fried shrimp, and that's that."

"Just a minute, Miss," the suitor said, motioning for the waitress to stay. He snipped off the end of a cigar and rolled it in his mouth, no doubt considering an investment. Then he looked at the boy, saying, "Son you can order anything on that menu that you want."

"I'll take a whole roasted duck!" the lad quickly said, smiling from ear to ear.

He got the whole duck platter, but I don't think he ever wanted another one. The teacher told me much later that the meat was awfully greasy, and, of course, the boy ate the whole thing, along with all of the stuffing and most of the trimmings.

Because ducks vary considerably in size as well as fat content, they often present a problem for the chef—and for the folks who feel obliged to eat the whole thing. Those epicures who have already become addicted to the rich dark meat of the duck will advise anyone, rather strongly, that the meat must be cooked rare. More squeamish folk don't want even a hint of pink showing in the meat. If you already have a favorite recipe for duck, use it when you are cooking for yourself. But when you have mixed company to feed, and want to avoid argument or disappointment from either side, forget about roasting the ducks. Dust off the old Dutch oven—and cook a gumbo. Here's what you'll need:

2 domestic ducks (5 pounds each, dressed weight)
2 cups duck stock (see below)
½ pound smoked beef sausage
5 or 6 slices of bacon
¼ cup bacon drippings (for roux)
¼ cup flour (for roux)
1 can stewed tomatoes (14½-ounce size)
1 can tomato paste (6-ounce size)
1 package frozen okra (10-ounce size) or fresh okra
8 ounces fresh mushrooms
2 stalks of celery, diced
2 medium onions, diced
2 cloves garlic, minced
½ large green bell pepper, diced
½ large red bell pepper, diced
1 tablespoon parsley
1 tablespoon chopped chives
4 small bay leaves
salt and pepper
rice (cooked separately)
filé (optional)

If the ducks are frozen, give them adequate time to thaw. Also thaw the okra. (About 2 cups of fresh okra, cut into wheels, is really better if you have it on hand.) Skin the duck and cut off the leg quarters. Separate the leg quarters into drumstick and thigh. Fillet the meat off both sides of the breast. Trim the fat off the pieces of breast, drumsticks, and thighs, wash them, and set them aside. Trim the fat off the backbone and rib sections, then put them into a large pot, along with the giblets and bay leaves. (It helps to break the duck's back in half so that the bones will fit into the pot easier.) Barely cover the bones with water. Bring to boil and simmer for at least 40 minutes, or until the meat pulls from the bones easily.

While waiting, make a dark roux in the Dutch oven. Start by frying the bacon until crisp and setting it aside to drain. Measure out ¼ cup of the bacon drippings and discard the rest. Heat to medium high and stir in the flour. Reduce heat to low and cook and stir, cook and stir, until the roux takes on a nice brown color.

In a separate pan, sauté the onions, pepper, and celery for 10 minutes in a little bacon grease. Remove, drain, and set aside. Sauté the okra for 10 minutes (add more drippings if needed). Put sautéed vegetables and crumbled bacon into the dutch oven with the roux. Mix in the duck breast, drumsticks, and thighs. Add tomatoes, parsley, salt, and pepper.

After the duck bones have simmered on the stove for 40 minutes or longer, add 2 cups of the broth to the Dutch oven. Bring almost to a boil, then cover and turn the heat to simmer.

Remove the bones from the boiling pot and pull the meat from them. Chop the meat, along with the giblets, and put it into the Dutch oven. Cut the beef sausage into bite-sized pieces and add to the gumbo. Cover tightly and simmer on very low heat for 3 or 4 hours. Stir from time to time with a wooden spoon. Lick the spoon after each stir.

Prepare the rice. Ladle the gumbo into individual bowls. If desirable, thicken the gumbo with a pinch or two of filé. (Proceed cautiously with the filé, adding it to individual serving bowls, not to the whole pot.) Add rice. Serves 8 or more.

Variations: There are thousands of gumbo recipes, all calling for different vegetables and different meats and seafoods. A duck gumbo, however, ought to have some duck in it, although you might want to add venison, cubed beef, or pork instead of sausage. Also, *any* gumbo ought to have a good bit of okra in it. On this I insist. In fact, the very word "gumbo" means "okra" in some West African dialects. The okra, being slightly mucilaginous, adds a certain texture that distinguishes a true gumbo from a thick soup or stew.

I hate to stir up any Cajuns, but they're going to be irritated at something anyhow, so I'll go ahead and say that both the roux and the filé are optional. The roux, often taken to the ritual stage, does add to the flavor and to the color of the gumbo, so I prefer to have it. The filé is, for the most part, a thickening agent, although some folks say it adds flavor. I usually omit it from my serving.

Wild duck variations: Wild ducks can be used in the above recipe, but remember that one kind of duck may be much larger than another. Small teal, fat mallards, and various ducks in between these two extremes are hard to compare in numbers. Also, ducks that have been feeding heavily on fish may require a marinade. (A simple marinade of ½ tablespoon of baking soda and ½ tablespoon of salt per quart of water can do wonders within 12 hours; in a glass or ceramic container, cover the duck with marinade and refrigerate it overnight.) Not all wild ducks, however, require a soak.

I've also cooked the above recipe with three large domestic ducks that had been robbed of the breast. The trick here is to fillet out the breast, getting two hand-sized pieces from each duck. (Put these aside for cooking the recipe below.) Skin out the rest of the duck, then disjoint the legs and thighs. Bone these and cube the meat. Cook the back, neck, etc., as indicated above. Use the boned legs and thighs instead of breast meat. There are any number of ways to use the breast of duck, but I recommended grilling it over charcoal, or over gas-heated or electrically-heated lava rocks. Here's a good one to try:

Grilled Duck Fillets

Prepare breast fillets (skinned) as described above. Allow at least two fillets (one breast) per person if you are using large domestic ducks. Several hours before cooking time, prepare a marinade by mixing

½ cup bacon drippings

½ cup red wine vinegar

2 tablespoons soy sauce

1 clove garlic, pressed

1 teaspoon lemon pepper seasoning salt

Put the duck breasts into a glass or crockery container and pour the marinade over them. Refrigerate for 2 or 3 hours, stirring once or twice. When you are ready to cook, build a hot charcoal fire (or heat the lava rocks) in a grill with a cover. Remove the duck breasts from the marinade; retain the liquid.

Place the duck breast fillets onto the rack, close hood, and grill for 5 minutes. Using tongs, dip each fillet quickly in the marinade liquid, then place back on grill, uncooked side down, of course. Close the cover and cook for 5 minutes. (Exact times are difficult to set forth because of variations in heat, distance from meat to heat, etc. For the very best flavor and texture, serve the fillets medium rare. When tested, they should be pinkish inside but should not ooze blood.) Serve fillets whole, like steaks, and provide a steak knife for each guest. Some folks will want a little more lemon pepper sprinkled on the breasts.

Variation: if you want more smoke flavor, cook the fillets under a closed hood and put some green hickory (or dry chips that have been soaked in water) or other good wood in with the charcoal or lava rocks.

One of the best ways to cook duck is in a thick soup with plenty of barley. This is a hearty dish, and I can make a meal from it:

Duck Soup with Barley

1 large domestic duck, fresh or frozen

1 cup pearl barley

3 stalks celery, finely chopped

1 medium onion, chopped

3 cloves garlic, minced

1 tablespoon chopped chives

½ teaspoon pepper

salt to taste

4 cups water

2 cups duck broth

½ cup red wine

3 bay leaves

If the duck is frozen, thaw it out. Skin the duck. Fillet out each side of the breast and set aside. Disjoint the rest of the duck, put it into a pot, cover with water, add 3 bay leaves, cover, and boil for an hour, or until tender. While the duck is boiling in the pot, cut the breast pieces into chunks, and put them into a Dutch oven. Add 4 cups water, pepper, chives, celery, onion, and garlic. (It's best to scrape the stalks of celery, then cut the stalks into several strips longways before chopping, making for smaller than usual pieces.) Put on low heat.

When the duck in the boiler is tender, after an hour or so, take it out and bone the meat. Chop the meat and giblets and add to the Dutch oven. Add two cups of the duck broth and discard the rest. Stir in a cup of pearl barley. Add ½ cup red wine. Bring to boil, reduce heat to low, cover, and simmer for 2 hours. Serve in bowls and eat hot with a good bread.

Warning: make sure that you don't add more than a cup of pearl barley—especially if you are not going to watch the pot closely. Barley soaks up lots of water and expands greatly. It may even push the top off the Dutch oven. After the barley has cooked for an hour or so, remember to check the liquid in the pot. Add a little water if needed.

The soup recipe above is also good when made with 2 or 3 guinea hens instead of a duck.

TEN STEPS TO A SUCCULENT VENISON ROAST

The proprietor of a large bass pro shop once told me that fishing tackle sales had plummeted. "All the bass boys," he explained, "are sitting up in pine trees looking for deer. I ought not to have given them your secret rock salt recipe!"

Well, the method of incrusting a piece of meat in rock salt before roasting it has been used since the 15th century, so it wasn't really mine. Further, the real secret of succulent venison goes far beyond a magic recipe. It's a ten-step process:

1. Climbing a pine tree isn't a bad way to start, if you've got a safe, adquate platform or stand mounted to it. You need a vantage from which you will be likely to have a clear view of your game. Whether you hunt from a tree stand or not, your hunting skill and knowledge of the white tail (or other game animals) will often get you a better shot at a prime animal.

When choosing a stand, also consider its location to your 4-wheeler or other vehicle, camp, or home. In short, remember that you'll have to get the deer out of the woods in a reasonable length of time, especially in warm or mild weather. Transporting the deer is discussed in more detail in step 4.

2. After you get an open shot, your marksmanship and equipment will determine how you follow through. Hit where you aim, so that you won't have a wounded deer

running all over the country. (Remember that knowledgeable farmers and meat butchers all over the world take precautions to kill hogs, sheep, cows, and goats as cleanly and quickly as possible.) If exactly on target, a head or neck shot with the proper load will result in a quick kill, but most modern experts agree that the odds are better, under most hunting conditions, if you will go for a heart and lung shot.

3. After you have dropped your deer, field dress it as soon as possible. Bleeding isn't necessary, especially if you have made a good lung shot. Hanging the animal by the hind legs isn't necessary either. Bleeding and hanging in the field usually take too much time—time that would be better spent by getting the insides out of the animal so that the meat will cool down faster. The bigger the animal, the more body heat it holds and the more important quick field dressing becomes.

To start field dressing a deer, turn it on its back. Cut through the hide and belly lining from the lower part of the breastbone down to the anus, being careful not to puncture any of the intestines or organs. Most people "tie off" the penis and rectum tubes with a piece of string and pull them through the opening in the pelvic bones. This practice permits one to field dress the animal without any sawing or cutting through bones. Remove the innards quickly, but carefully. Remember that deer don't have gall bladders, so you don't have to worry when removing the liver. Pull all the innards out. Cut around the lungs and chest tissues. Reach high into the chest cavity and sever the tubes in the throat. Pull all the chest organs and belly innards out and pull the deer away from them. Prop the cut open with a couple of sticks, allowing air to circulate in the cavity. After you have the innards out, you can hang the deer up to cool if you are to be in the woods for a long period or time, or you can start transporting the field dressed meat immediately.

I might add that a good, sharp knife is very important when field dressing a deer. In fact, I recommend that you take two knives, both with a 3- to 3½-inch blade. A simple drop-point blade design is my favorite for all purpose use. A special skinning knife is nice to have, but remember that skinning the deer in the field is not usually recommended for white tail. This advice may not always hold for bear and some other big game.

A few people might still worry about tarsal glands on the animal's hind legs. The main thing to know about tarsal glands is their location. In short, know where they are—and leave them alone. Merely cut off the lower no-meat leg at the joint and discard it. Don't try to cut the gland out. Tarsal stink is the last thing you want on your knife blade when field dressing or butchering a deer.

4. One person, in good health and hearty condition, can drag a deer for a considerable distance, but two people are much better for this task. The deer can be pulled along the ground, which can result in some damage to the meat, or it can be put onto some sort of frame and either carried or dragged. Some people shoulder a small deer, which is fine if you are man enough. Just remember to put some bright orange flagging onto the antlers. Lots of flagging.

If a motor vehicle is available, avoid putting the deer across the hood. Heat from the engine can ruin the meat. In cold weather, freezing the meat during transport and then having to thaw it out for butchering is not good for the meat.

5. Hanging or curing a carcass for a few days at the proper temperature and humidity will often help the flavor and texture of some meats, including venison. If you don't have personal access to proper cooling facilities, your best bet will be to take your deer to a professional meat processor. Do this as soon as possible. Let a pro age the deer,

butcher it, and package it for your freezer. If you hang your own, at home or in camp, try to avoid temperature extremes. In order words, don't let the deer freeze at night and thaw out in the day. Also remember that blow flies and other insects can be a problem, so use a good but well-ventilated game bag or other other means of protecting the carcass. Rather than hang the meat in unsuitable conditions, it would be better to skin it immediately, cut it into sections, and store it in ice chests for a few days. Most of the deer that I eat are in fact cured at home in ice chests.

In any case, proper butchering helps venison. I prefer to bone the shoulders and roll the meat into roasts. With hind quarters, I usually separate the muscles at their natural divisions. This process reduces a large hind quarter to small roasts. My thinking is that the smaller the roast, the easier it is to cook. Also remember that you can slice the smaller roasts into steaks or "cutlets."

Before you butcher your meat, you might consider all the previous steps listed above. If your animal was not killed cleanly, and was not field dressed quickly, you might consider cutting the whole thing up into stew meat or grinding it into burger meat. In any case, only prime meat should be cooked as a roast.

6. Most of the meat taken from deer, elk, or other big game goes into a home freezer. Provided that the meat is properly wrapped, freezing is good for the meat. In fact, prime venison that has been properly field dressed can go directly into a freezer without hanging it or aging it in any other way. I prefer to keep frozen, uncured venison a month or so before eating it. (How long *can* you keep it? I don't know, but I try to clean out my freezer each year before a new hunting season starts.)

7. If your venison is frozen, be sure to remove it from the freezer early enough for it to thaw out before the cook-

ing adventure begins, unless of course you've got a recipe that will work with frozen meat. I often let meat thaw at room temperature, and I sometimes put it under running water of mild temperature. But thawing a roast overnight in a refrigerator is usually the best procedure. Overnight thawing can, however, cause a timing problem, especially if you also want to marinate the meat.

Really good meat doesn't require a marinade, unless you are preparing a dish like sauerbraten, where the flavor of a marinade is necessary for the success of the recipe. But I do marinate meat quite often in ordinary milk. When meat seems a little strong to the nose, I use a marinade made with 1 tablespoon of ordinary baking soda per quart of water. In any case, I am guilty of putting a frozen roast in a marinade and letting it thaw overnight in the refrigerator. One firm rule: Never marinate meat in a metal container. Use glass, crockery, or even plastic.

8. At one time, putting beef suet or other fat into lean meat was a common practice and special "barding" or "larding" needles were standard tools for the complete chef. Modern practitioners, however, usually make do with inserting pieces of bacon or salt pork into a slit in the meat, or by wrapping the meat with strips of bacon. Also, strips of bacon can be rolled up inside roasts that have been boned. After rolling, the roast is tied with cotton strings.

No doubt barding and larding will make the meat more moist, but it also helps defeat one main advantage of eating venison in the first place. Venison is believed to be healthy, partly because it is low in fat. And, if it is properly cooked, it can be quite succulent without barding and larding.

I don't even own a larding or barding needle, but I do often use a trick with garlic that I learned from my wife, who says she got it from an Armenian peasant. Here's how it's done: Using your thinnest fillet knife, make a narrow slit deep into the roast. Peel a clove of garlic and slice it in half, lengthwise. Insert the garlic pieces, one after the other, into the slit. During cooking, the garlic seems to keep the meat from drying out. The flavor that the garlic imparts to the meat is not too strong—and even the garlic itself has a pleasantly mild taste after it is cooked inside a roast.

9. As a rule, cooking ground meat and stew meat (cut into chunks) is easier than cooking whole roasts. But, somehow, there's nothing quite like serving up a roast to guests. It's something visual, I suppose. But it can backfire on you if the roast isn't good. Any roast, if cooked too long, is likely to be far too dry, and tough. This is especially true with venison, which tends to be on the lean side to start with, as compared to beef that has been penned up and fattened for market.

The key to cooking succulent roast is having the right temperature (usually in an oven) for the right length of time. Unfortunately, this varies from one piece of meat to another. Further, some ovens are not accurate, and even the position of the meat in the oven can be important. For all these reasons, I highly recommend that you use a meat thermometer. Get a good one. After all, the meal you are about to cook is the culmination of the hunt, which probably cost some money in equipment, time, and transportation. Why skimp on the price of a meat thermometer?

Using your favorite venison roast recipe, first preheat the oven. Then insert the meat thermometer into the center of the roast. (If your roast has a bone in it, the thermometer should not touch it.) Put the roast in the center of the preheated oven. Set the oven timer for the minimum length recommended by your recipe—but check the thermometer once or twice before the end of the time period. When the temperature inside the roast reaches 130 degrees, your roast is medium rare; 135 to 145 degrees, medium; 150 degrees, medium well; over 160 degrees, well done. I recommend 130 degrees. Anyone at the table who doesn't like medium rare meat can usually be fed off either end of the roast. Some people object to a little blood oozing onto the plate from rare or medium rare meat. This can be minimized, without overcooking, by letting the roast sit for a few minutes before carving it.

If you want to try my rock salt method of cooking a roast, purchase at least five or six pounds of ordinary ice cream salt. Preheat your oven to 450 degrees. Select a roasting pan large enough for the roast, with plenty of room all around. (I usually use an oven-proof ceramic dish, which is attractive enough to put onto the table.) Line the bottom of the pan with an inch of rock salt. Pepper the roast all around, then carefully insert the thermometer. Place the roast onto the rock salt in the roasting pan, turning so that the thermometer sticks straight up. Slowly pour salt around the roast, working upward. Go slowly until the entire roast is covered with at least ½-inch of rock salt. Then put the roast into the center of the preheated oven. Cook for half an hour, then start checking the thermometer from time to time. Cook until the thermometer reads 130 degrees, then remove the roast from the oven. It can sit aside for a while, but it should be served while still hot. How you serve the meat is, of course, quite important to success, as discussed in the next step.

10. Even a rather mundane venison roast can be made into a memorable experience by the right atmosphere, setting, and company. An open hearth fire or candlelight can work wonders for lovers, where there is already a natural attraction. But non-magnetic guests, especially old hunting pals and their reluctant spouses, may require some showmanship. Start with giving your guests something that is easy to remember—such as a venison roast cooked inside a mound of rock salt. If you've got a gift for gab, you might invent a story about Henry VIII, or somebody, cooking in this manner a roast off a royal stag.

Cheap trick or not, I almost always leave the venison roast encased in the rock salt mound when I put it onto the table. Before my guests the salt is cracked off ceremoniously, usually by tapping it with the blunt end of a table knife until the mound cracks and then meticulously pulling the segments off in small pieces. Any remaining salt can be brushed off with the hand. Then the meat is transferred from the roasting pan to a serving platter.

After the rock salt and roasting pan have been removed from the table, the carving can begin. Put on a show if you are so inclined. One trick that seems to work in the mind of your guests is to swish a carving knife back and forth against a sharpening steel. Just don't get carried away and cut your finger off, especially if you've been heavily testing the proof of the ingredient used in the next show.

For some guests, I enjoy flaming a venison roast with brandy. Sometimes I flame the whole roast, but more often I work with slices that have been put into a warmed platter. In either case, I heat a little brandy in a sauce pan, pour it over the roast, and ignite it with a long match. Usually, I dim the lights before flaming.

Whether or not you flame the meat, serve it with a colorful salad, vegetables of your choice, and hearty bread. I recommend a tossed salad with oil and vinegar dressing, with plenty of very ripe tomato wedges in it, along with vivid green peppers, and a black olive or two along with lettuce and other salad stuffs. In other words, go for color as well as taste. Also, a few last-minute twists of freshly-ground black pepper from a hand mill will add an aroma as well as flavor.

For vegetables, try steamed carrots or cauliflower, and baked potatoes. If you've got fresh mushrooms, sauté them for a few minutes in butter, then flame them along with the meat. For bread, a long loaf of San Francisco style sour dough, properly buttered and browned, is both colorful and tasty. The drink? With venison I like a good red wine. Enjoy.

* * *

Once I was floating the lazy Suwannee River in Florida, plugging the likely spots for a small, blue-bellied bass that grows there. It was a damp, cold day, more suitable for duck hunting than for bait-casting, and my fishing buddy and I did more silent drifting than fishing. Just as I was about to make a cast to an eddy behind a large rock, my partner nudged me and pointed his rod to a couple wearing blaze orange pull-down caps in a palmetto deer stand. "The best way to hunt deer," he whispered, "is to take a woman with you." Maybe he was right. If so, the best way to start would be to dine her on a rock salt venison roast, meticulously prepared from start to finish.

GUINEA HEN ON THE MIND

Carl Barber and his sister, Marion, gave a sort of dinner party one night. Suspecting nothing, I went because I needed food, company, talk, and a drink or two. Besides, Marion had a knack for gathering interesting people, and she had invited a female mathematician, a frisky German rocket scientist, a male nurse, a scholar who was doing a book on Celtic music, and so on. It truly was an assorted group, and even included an elderly Episcopalian preacher, who seemed to be sleepy.

Barber seated me between two painted and highly powdered women of middle age, both with wigs and big bosoms. Quickly I surmised from the shoptalk between them that the one on my left sold Avon products, and that the one on my right sold Tupperware products. Quickly I realized that I was caught between these two jabbering women. Barber grinned at me from across the table, and I knew that he had set me up.

"Madames!" I thought, practicing my lines and, in my mind's eye, banging on the table for attention. "Madames, I'll thank you to quit jabbering in my ears." The word "jabbering" wasn't strong enough for what I wanted to say. "Madames! Silence! Silence I say! Silence at the board!" Maybe, I thought, I ought to make a grand exit.

But I said nothing, did nothing. As the dinner moved along, the other guests struck up conversations about mathematics and sex and music and rocketry and other interesting topics, causing Avon and Tupperware to go at it ever louder and louder and to stick their heads closer and closer together in order to talk sales and motivational tactics. They almost touched bosoms over my plate, and I started inching my chair back. Barber grinned.

Marion, always the gracious hostess, sat a new platter of fried meat on the table, asking me to be sure to try it. I couldn't make out what exactly it was. The golden brown pieces weren't large enough to be drumsticks. Quickly Carl pushed the platter down the table a ways, as if he didn't want me to have any. "Excuse me, Ladies," I said, parting their heads and reaching for a piece or two of the fried food. It was very, very good. It tasted like fried chicken. It crunched like fried chicken. It looked like fried chicken. But it simply wasn't a drumstick. I ate three or four.

"What are these, Carl?" I asked, taking some more.

"Guinea legs," he said. He didn't say it loudly, but I read his lips.

I took another bite or two, looking closely at the meat. It was quite white, and tender. And mild of flavor. I had eaten guinea several times, but it had been a long time ago. "Did you say guinea legs? I thought that guinea meat was sort of dark," I said, "and maybe a little . . . strong isn't the word. Gamey? Like dove, maybe." He didn't answer. I ate another piece or two. "These are *very* good," I said. "Where did you get them?"

"Got'em on the way back," he said.

"Back from where?" I asked after a while. Listening carefully for his answer, I cocked my head a bit and elbowed my way in between Avon and Tupperware. "Excuse me, Ladies," I said, hitching my chair up to the table. They moved over an inch or so but didn't even slow down. "Back from where?" I asked, louder now, thinking that maybe I could buy some for myself.

"Waterloo," Carl said. "We went to Waterloo Sunday, and I picked them up on the way back."

"Picked them up from *where*, exactly?" I asked. He was from Quitman, Georgia.

He didn't answer.

"There must be a hundred legs there," I said. "That's a lot of guinea hens."

"Fifty, to be exact," he said.

"Where in the hell are you gonna get 50 guinea hens?" I asked, determined to pin him down.

"A farmer over toward Waterloo raises 'em," he said. "Sells the feathers to a fellow down in Louisiana. Ever hear of the Green Trout Guinea? A fishing lure. Made with guinea feathers. It's hell on bass. Takes a lot of guineas to meet the fishing lure demand, and this farmer over toward Waterloo raises 'em commercially. A restaurant out of New Orleans buys the breasts and the farmer gets rid of the rest of the guinea meat the best way he can. I usually buy thighs, but he didn't have anything left except legs when we stopped by Sunday. He had a few wings and necks, but of course guinea wings and necks really don't have enough meat on 'em to fool with."

"Of course not," I said, reaching for more. I was getting quite a pile of guinea leg bones on my plate by now. "I'll tell you," I said, pushing the bones aside, "these are much better than chicken legs."

Well, suddenly Barber broke out laughing. He couldn't quit. His sister, a little embarrassed now at her brother's crude manners, got a big bowl and came around with it, giving everybody a big helping of what she called dumplings and wing tips. The talk resumed as she made her way around the table, and my ears buzzed again with Avon and Tupperware talk. When the hostess got to me, I looked into the dumpling bowl and saw that the bigger part of the wings had been removed. Then I realized that I had been taken by Carl Barber. Just to be sure, I took a big helping from the dumpling bowl, quickly isolated a half wing that was pretty much intact, and fitted a 'guinea leg' bone up against it. A perfect match.

Carl started laughing again. Then he started flopping his elbows about and tried to go like a chicken, right at the table. The laughing turned into a sort of dry gasping sound, deep from the belly, and he toppled out of the chair, balled up. If his condition caused concern at the table, I couldn't hear or see it because of Avon and Tupperware.

Suddenly I parted the wig-haired heads and pushed the women out of my way, stood up, and banged on the table loudly enough to hush the company and bring Carl's head up above the table. Even Avon and Tupperware fell silent, their mouths open, and the preacher woke up just as I shouted, "Barber! You dirty son-of-a-bitch! Quitman, Georgia, is the gnat capitol of the world!"

Years later, somebody started beating on my front door one morning before the crack of day. As soon as I switched on the lamp beside the bed, my wife turned to the wall and covered her head with a pillow. She mumbled something about Henry. It was Saturday, the day of our two-man bass tournament, and no doubt Henry had stayed up all night trying to figure out a way to beat me. I admit that I had stayed up late myself, but I finally dozed off at around 3:30 in the morning. I hadn't been asleep long when Henry started knocking on the front door.

I let him in. Before long I had coffee perking and sausage sizzling on the griddle. I knew, of course, that Henry would start fishing right away.

"If I were you," he said, making his first cast from the stool he had taken at my breakfast bar, "I would cook that sausage well done. There have been some cases of trichinosis around here lately. You eat a lot of pork, don't you? I mean, have you been feeling all right? Look, if you don't feel like fishing today──"

"Don't worry," I said, knowing that he had been reading in his copy of *Gamesmanship* again. Or the psychology book. "This isn't pork sausage," I added, taking up a link with tongs and placing it onto a brown grocery bag to drain. Nothing is better for draining fried fish or sausage than ordinary brown bags.

"Well . . . what sort of sausage is it?" he asked, finally.

"Half armadillo."

"Yeah? That ought to be pretty good. What's the other half, if you don't mind my asking?"

"Muskrat. Ground it up myself. Of course, I put lots of seasoning and hot stuff in the ground meat and I used genuine hog guts for the casing, not that plastic stuff. Nothing beats genuine hog guts for sausage casing early in the morning. Funny thing about those hog guts. You know that pet shoat that Dow Jones raised for his kids? A fat little ol' Poland China, white with black spots. With a cute little curly tail. A personable hog."

"I know exactly which goddamn hog you're talking about," he said. "Just cook the sausage, Doctor."

"Eggs?" I asked, feeling one-up already, before we had even wet a line. The chicken eggs looked kind of small this morning, about like pullet eggs, so I got 7 or 8 of 'em out of the carton.

"I'm not very hungry, so 4 or 5 of those little ol' things will do me," he said, watching me as I broke some eggs onto the griddle. They sizzled for a minute. Then, just as I surehandedly scooped up an egg with my spatula, he said, "Doctor, you better cook those eggs over well." (He knew that I liked mine sunny-side up.) "They've had some bad cases of salmonella around here lately. Coming from chicken eggs. Bad stuff. Puts spots on your liver like rabbit fever. You better wash your hands real good."

"Yeah, I read about that," I said, carefully sliding the egg onto the brown bag, perfectly sunny-side up. "That's why my wife and I switched to these little guinea hen eggs here a while back. Guinea eggs are a little small, but boy are they good. Guinea hens of course don't eat anything except worms and June bugs and such, so there's nothing to worry about. No sir, you can't pen raise guinea hens on laying mash. Won't produce. Eggs that is. Won't lay. No way. Get a guinea egg and you've got the real thing. See that yellow eye in that egg?" I pointed the black end of my spatula at the yellow eye in the white circle on the brown paper. "You won't see a chicken egg with an eye like that."

"You're shitting me, Doctor," he said. "Where are you going to get guinea eggs?"

"Got 'em on the way back," I said, cracking another egg. The heat to my griddle was just right now, and the egg started turning white around the edges almost immediately.

"Back from where?" he asked.

"We went over to Waterloo Friday," I said. Luckily for my story in progress, I remembered that my wife had purchased a very large package of wingettes, or what I now called Carl Barber drumsticks. She had put them into the marinade crock, getting ready to cook a meal for several school teachers that we had invited over for an evening meal. "Look here," I said, getting the large crock out of the refrigerator. "Here's a few guinea legs that we brought back with us," I said, tilting the crock over so that he could see in.

"Well I'll be damned," he said, looking into the crock. "There must be a hundred drumsticks in here. That's a lot of flapping guineas."

"Fifty, to be exact," I said, putting the crock back into the refrigerator.

"My god, where you gonna find fifty guinea hens?"

"I got 'em on the way back, when we picked up the guinea eggs."

"*Where*, goddamnit," he said.

"A fellow named Barber raises them over toward Waterloo," I said. Then I asked, "Did you read that article on the nutritional advantages of guinea meat as compared to fatty, pen raised chickens?"

"No, I didn't read the article, Doctor, but I'll have you know that I've been eating guinea meat all my life. It sure as hell beats chicken."

Holding a straight face, I poured three cups of coffee, knowing that my wife would be in for some. She can't resist the smell of my coffee early in the morning. A special brew, part chickory, part coffee. Sure enough, she came right on, tucking in the tie strings on her pink robe, as soon as I started clanking the sugar spoon against the side of the cup while stirring.

"Well good morning," Henry said, standing up as if he were a gentleman. "I'm sorry that we woke you up."

"No the hell you're not," I said, distributing the cups of coffee around the table. "You did it on purpose."

"The smell of sausage frying is too tempting," my good wife said, breaking off a bite of mine. "This Gullage sausage is hard to beat."

"Pops and crackles, too," I said, quickly. "Sizzles is the word."

"*Gullage sausage?*" Henry said, jerking his head toward me. Silence. "I suppose you picked it up on the way back?"

"Back from where?" my wife asked.

"What do you think the bass will be hitting today, Honey?" I asked, quickly trying to change the subject. "I've designed a top secret spoon. It wobbles. It dives. It crawls——"

"I reckon it's dressed with guinea feathers," Henry said, raising his voice. I drew back the spatula in self defense, but he didn't get off the stool.

"I'm not playing any fishing games with you two boys this morning," she said, taking another bite of Gullage sausage. She headed back for the bed, taking her coffee with her. She stuck her head back through the doorway, saying, "Would you mind stirring those chicken wings for me? They're in the big brown marinade crock in the refrigerator."

"Stirring *what?*" Henry asked.

"Chicken wings," she said. "Wingettes."

She shut the bedroom door again, leaving the two of us eating sausage and drinking chickory coffee, head to head. He scraped the burned part off another piece of toast without speaking. He ate it, then drank off his coffee, still without speaking.

I broke the silence, asking, "Henry, did I understand you to say that guinea legs are better than chicken wings?"

"Let's go fishing, you dirty son-of-a-bitch," he said, sliding off the stool and heading for the door, "and I'll show you a thing or two."

Outside in the early morning air, I had an urge to flap my arms and crow like Carl Barber used to do. But I decided to hold it in until we got on the lake. Crowing during the day at 10, 2, and 4 would, I figured, greatly improve my chances of beating Henry at the fine game of bass fishing.

COLD TURKEY AT GOOSE BAY

Steady Eddie was a hell of a skeet shot. He got in lots of practice with his 12 gauge Browning over-and-under, shooting right off the bow of our ship while we plied the rough waters of the North Atlantic or lay at anchor in some remote, frigid bay. Since he was gunnery officer as well as the skipper of the U.S.S. Canyon, he could, I suppose, shoot all the skeet he wanted to shoot. He also enjoyed shelling icebergs from time to time with our 5-inch cannon.

But what about the rest of the crew? The Navy had sent the Canyon into these icy waters three summers in a row, doing secret missions in and around Greenland, Newfoundland, and Labrador. We would set sail (or get up steam) for these northern places from the port of Norfork, Virginia, which, at that time, was in itself no great shakes of a liberty town. We would stay up north for 2 or 3 months, then steam back to Norfork. It was a boring routine, and the crew got pretty much fed up with it during the third summer. Being ordinary sailors, we couldn't shoot at icebergs or practice skeet. We could play poker, but within a day or so after payday only a few of us had gambling money left. We could catch codfish by the thousands, but this also got boring after so many weeks; unlike some of the officers, we couldn't use the captain's gig or other small boats to go after more sporting species of fish, or the huge halibut, that swam these waters. It's true that we were allowed to head for the beach on landing craft from time to time to play baseball on the rocks, but the real purpose of these recreational trips was to drink beer. Yes, we did have beer aboard the Canyon. But we *always* had to go ashore to drink it and *always* under the guise of a ball game or some sort of recre-

78

ational jaunt, and, sometimes, on photographic sessions for those among us who had, or could borrow, a camera. Film wasn't necessary.

One day, Steady Eddie went ashore to play baseball with the boys and he saw with his own eyes that there wasn't a place flat enough to level a ping pong table on, much less to lay out a baseball diamond of suitable size. A quick thinker, he decided on the spot to change the Sport of the Day from baseball to mountain climbing, and he was to lead the first party. From the beach he eyed a pretty good foothill and set out for it.

Before the mountain climbing party got anywhere close to the top of the first peak, however, they ran out of beer. Steady Eddie sent a work detail of four men back to the ship for more beer, and the rest of the party waited, finishing off what little brew they had left. They waited. And they waited. Without beer. Finally, Steady Eddie sent a four-man search detail to look for the beer detail. What was left of the mountain climbing party waited. And they waited. Finally, Steady Eddie himself led the party back to the ship and organized search parties to look for the beer detail and the search detail. The next day, they found both details holed up in a cave. These brave men had survived the ordeal only by having the presence of mind to drink the beer for its caloric survival value.

Not long after the men were rescued, we upped anchor and steamed far north to another bay. There was an Eskimo village near our new anchorage, or so we had been told by a fur-lined fellow in a kayak who bummed sea-duty cigarettes from the ship's crew. Of course everybody realized that such a small village, maybe of 100, simply would not support ship's liberty. There wasn't even a bar.

In any case, the village was quickly put off-limits to baseball players, mountain climbers, photographers, and all other sailors. But it wasn't off the mind. Bit by bit the imagined joys of an ice palace grew, and ordinary igloos became pleasures domes, until one night a gang of six lowered the Captain's gig, climbed down a shaky rope ladder, and made off for the beach, braving the choppy waters, cold and rough, of the North Atlantic. And the darkness. God, it was dark up there. The gang of sailors found the village without mishap, and, to make a long story short, they literally tore the place up. But they managed to get back aboard the Canyon without being discovered. The captain's gig floated away. At least, that's the story. And it was true that the captain's gig *was* missing—and that's partly what made Steady Eddie so mad.

He held an enquiry. Of course, nobody knew anything— or wouldn't talk—and Steady Eddie felt that he had no choice but to crack down on the whole crew. First, he put a stop to all mountain climbing until such time as somebody should come forth with information. That didn't help. Next, he stopped all baseball games. That didn't help, either. Next, the photographic sessions were stopped, along with all beer-accompanied trips ashore, for whatever reason. This produced some grumbling, but nobody squealed on those who had jumped ship, if indeed anybody could put a finger on the guilty sailors. And it is entirely possible that nobody jumped ship at all. Some of us believed that the Eskimos framed the U.S. Navy, stealing the Captain's gig and claiming all sorts of property damage as well as various violations of the flesh. But if Steady Eddie ever considered this possibility, I wasn't privy to his thoughts.

The worst was yet to come. When Steady Eddie's enquiries didn't produce names or even information, he took it upon his rank to cut off all coffee rations to all spaces except for the mess halls, where coffee would be served once a day, at breakfast. Now this was serious business. You can't run a Navy without coffee. Who will stand the midnight watch? The system simply won't work without plenty of coffee. Why, every space and every hole aboard a U.S. Navy ship has its own coffee pot. In the engineering section where I worked, for example, we had a coffee pot in both the port and starboard engine rooms, as well as in the two boiler rooms and all other engineering spaces except the log room and shaft alley. In the engine room, as I have stated before, there was nothing to do except sit on an oil can and drink coffee and smoke and tell salty tales of Singapore or Naples.

For a week we suffered, carefully eking out what little coffee we had on hand. For 10 days we held on. Then, one night, somebody—and I honestly don't know who—took an oxyacetylene torch and cut a hole through the steel bulkhead leading to the commissary store room. In the dark of night the hot sparks flew. Whoever did this deed made away with 800 pounds of coffee and 92 gallons of canned turkey. (The coffee, if I remember correctly, was packed in 50-pound bags, and missing were 40 bags. The turkey was in gallon tins packed four per case, making 23 cases.) The word of the theft quickly got out, and most of us, sensing impending disciplinary action, hid what little coffee we had on hand.

But nothing happened, and there was only silence from the bridge. Steady Eddie didn't talk about the theft. The Commissary Officer didn't talk about it. The Chief Master-at-Arms didn't talk about it. What information we got, we knew, was pure scuttlebutt. But we knew as absolute fact that some naval Robbing Hood was doling out coffee and turkey to the crew. Of these good deeds we received proof positive. One dark night someone left, at the bottom of the ladder leading down into our engine room, a 50 pound bag of coffee and a gallon can of turkey. But nothing was said.

During the silence, however, Steady Eddie was planning his move. Early one morning he struck. All hands were ordered to stand by their work stations for roll call and inspection in dress uniform. Well, breaking out dress blues and shining shoes in the middle of Goose Bay, a thousand miles from a liberty town, didn't set well with the crew.

One disgruntled Boatswain's Mate, I understand, lined up in faded denim work clothes and unpolished brown loafer shoes instead of the regulation Navy black and spit shine. But I didn't see it. All I know is that our crew for the Port Engine Room assembled in front of the throttle board for muster, stood at attention, and waited. And waited. Before long, we all fell out, got out the oil cans, and took a seat. After several hours, word came around, however, that the Captain, the Master at Arms, the Commissary Officer, and a string of other officers were inspecting the Canyon, one hole at a time. Hup-to.

A Machinist's Mate called Screws had rigged a hidden refrigerator for the engine-room crew. If I remember correctly, this ingenious fellow, who always had dirty hands and seldom went topside, actually made the refrigerator from an old air compressor that he found in a salvage pile at the Boston shipyard. He installed it cleverly inside a steel tool cabinet underneath a work bench. A false wall could be pulled out, opening up an insulated space suitable for keeping coffee cream, snacks, fresh codfish, cold drinks, and so on. The refrigerator's compressor had been wired into an electrical supply line, and it had a concealed switch. Of course, we shut the motor off, not wanting it to kick in during Steady Eddie's inspection.

Our coffee pot was also near the refrigerator, on top of the work bench. Screws had made it also, and it was heated by steam. 'Twas a beautiful thing with a stainless steel jacket and polished brass stopcock. Of course, we drained out the coffee and dried the pot long before Steady Eddie's inspection party got to the port engine room.

By throwing out some foodstuff we managed to pack the 50-pound bag of coffee beans into the refrigerator. Our plan was, if discovered, to claim that the coffee had been saved up from our daily rations. To prove otherwise would be difficult. The turkey was something that couldn't be explained, since it wasn't rationed in any way, and was under the control of Commissary. So, we took the head off a steam-powered cooling water pump, inserted the gallon can inside the cylinder, and closed it up with nuts and bolts. So, we were ready for most anything.

When Steady Eddie descended the ladder, followed by his retinue, we stood by, watching the ladder that led down into our space. First appeared Steady Eddie's brown shoes, his brown pants, his brown coat, and, finally, his brown cap with scrambled-eggs gold braid on the visor. We had lined up along the throttle board. After being saluted and welcomed to the Port Engine Room, Steady Eddie made a quick review of the men, snorted, and immediately went on down another ladder to the lower deck. Immediately behind the Captain were two enlisted men bearing flash lights, brought along, no doubt, to do the dirty work, like going into the bilge. One of these grinned at us, and the other winked and shook his head, indicating that thus far the inspection party had found no coffee or turkey. The rest of the officers followed by rank, winding around like a snake. The commissary officer came last. Well, the search party looked in every hole on the lower deck, on top of every steam line, behind the reduction gear housing, atop the pumps, behind the steam lines, behind the turbine insulation—everywhere. They even looked and poked around in the bilges, shining lights about.

Finding nothing below, they came up and gave the top level a going over. Steady Eddie paused beside the tool cabinet, opened the door, and felt around inside, but he didn't sense that it had a false wall. Among the tools he found our cast-iron frying pan that we used to cook freshly caught codfish. By way of explanation, one of our quick-thinking petty officers said he wasn't sure, but he thought the frying pan had been used to melt lead to repair plumbing during the years of the great war. This was a joke, really, because our high-pressure steam would have melted the lead. But Steady Eddie seemed satisfied with the explanation. In any case, he checked his watch, wheeled, and headed back up the ladder. First the scrambled-egg hat disappeared through the hole in the next deck. Then the jacket. Then the pants. Then the shoes. The two enlisted men with flashlights and the other officers followed, disappearing one by one. The Commissary Officer brought up the rear. First went his hat. His jacket. Pants. (It was almost over now.) Brown shoes—

Suddenly, Screws said, "Would you fellows like to have a cup of coffee and a turkey sandwich before you leave?"

We all froze. The Commissary Officer froze, with only his brown shoes showing. For what seemed a very long while the shoes remained on the rung of the ladder. Then he eased on up without a word.

Later, we learned that the party found not a single gallon of turkey and not a single bean of coffee aboard the Canyon. They did, however, discover an unclaimed cask of raisinjack in the gyrocompass room. For the next week, nobody received any new ration of coffee grounds. Nobody needed any. For the port engine room, for example, we had 50 pounds of coffee and a gallon of cold turkey—enough to last us until Steady Eddie weighed anchor and headed the Canyon back for Norfork, full speed ahead.

Thus, I learned how to make cold turkey sandwiches while serving my country in what we called the Battle of Goose Bay. Furthermore, turkey is turkey, whether it be in Goose Bay or Lexington or San Diego. Let's face it. There's not much you can do for the turkey meat after it has been baked or canned, and most Thanksgiving birds around the country are cooked far too long in the first place. By far the best course is to make turkey sandwiches. If it were up to me, turkey would be eaten in no other way. When making a palatable turkey sandwich, however, a good deal depends on the bread and the mayonnaise.

Of course, we had plenty of bottled mayonnaise (or maybe salad dressing) aboard the Canyon, but it was kept under lock and key in a refrigeration compartment. We didn't want to risk an oxyacetylene torch operaton, just for a gallon jug of mayonnaise, however, and we didn't have any trustworthy contacts. Our concern was that anyone caught stealing mayonnaise might be tied to the great turkey and coffee theft. And of course our engine-room boys didn't actually steal the turkey or the coffee. We were guilty only of consuming evidence.

Fortunately, one of our engine room crew was Italian and he claimed to know how to make mayonnaise that would be much better than sea rations. The secret recipe had been passed on to him from his father, who in turn learned it from his grandfather. He needed eggs, however. Somebody traded a carton of Camel cigarettes to the Eskimos for a dozen or so very small chicken eggs. At least, he *said* they were chicken eggs. The Italian also needed lemon juice and a little powdered mustard, along with sugar and pepper and a few other items that were easily obtained. The lemons, I understand, came from the Officers Mess, although I don't know how—and I didn't want to know at the time. For confectioner's sugar, he pounded a little ordinary sugar until it was as fine as powder. One key ingredient—olive oil—came from the Italian's personal stock. Here's pretty much what we used and what you'll need:

Mayonnaise

yolks from 3 pullet eggs or 2 medium hen eggs
1 cup olive oil (used in two batches)
*2 tablespoons lemon juice plus ½ teaspoon lemon
    juice*
1½ tablespoons vinegar
½ teaspoon dry mustard

½ teaspoon salt

½ teaspoon confectioner's sugar

⅛ teaspoon finely ground pepper (white, if available)

⅛ teaspoon paprika (if available)

Build a suitable wire whisk or carve out a wooden spoon. Set out all ingredients, and a suitable bowl or non-metallic container, so that they will reach room temperature (about 70 degrees). Separate the egg whites and yolks. Put the yolks into the bowl and mix in the dry mustard, salt, pepper, confectioner's sugar, and ½ teaspoon of lemon juice. While beating the mixture, slowly, very slowly, add ½ cup of the olive oil. Whisk the mixture until it begins to thicken.

In a cup, mix the vinegar and 2 tablespoons of lemon juice. Have the rest of the olive oil at hand in another cup. Very, very slowly stir in a few drops of the vinegar and lemon juice, then stir in a few drops of olive oil, while beating constantly. Repeat the process until all the lemon juice, vinegar, and oil are used up. If all goes well, you'll have a smooth, thick sauce that spreads nicely and tastes wonderful. Immediately put this mixture into a refrigerator, or on ice, and keep it cool until you are ready to make turkey sandwiches. Also chill the turkey, canned or not. Here's what you'll need:

Cold Turkey Sandwiches

cold turkey

white bread

mayonnaise

black pepper

Chill the turkey and mayonnaise. Get some good white bread, soft, very soft, and slice it a little thick. In Goose Bay, we knew a baker aboard the Canyon, and he provided a fresh loaf every night. I believe that something about the way we sliced it with a hacksaw blade made the bread even better. I'll call it the rough-cut factor. But if you don't make your own bread, try the regular white bread from the grocery store or bakery, but not the thin sandwich slices. Get two pieces of bread and spread each slice generously with the mayonnaise.

Slice the turkey thin. Cut some slices with the grain and some against the grain, giving a variety in texture. I use a fillet knife for this purpose, but any good knife will do. Pile the turkey high onto one piece of bread, using six or seven slices, then sprinkle with pepper to taste. Top with the other piece of bread. Use no lettuce, no pickles, or other such stuff. Just make sure that you've got very soft bread with plenty of mayonnaise on it.

Cut the sandwich in half, diagonally. Go ahead. Take the first bite right out of the middle.

HOW TO BOIL SHRIMP
IMPECCABLY

At sea level, water boils at 212 degrees, a perfect temperature for cooking shrimp. But being at the right altitude guarantees nothing except constant temperature of the boil, and, by the same token, being in Denver doesn't make things entirely hopeless. The secret to cooking good shrimp consistently is having *enough* very hot water as compared to the volume of shrimp. Bringing a little water to a roaring boil, then cooling it down quickly by dumping in a large batch of ice-cold shrimp, simply will not do. On the other hand, if you have lots of boiling water, it won't cool down too much when you dump the shrimp into it. Then you can cook the shrimp quickly.

How quickly? Two minutes for small shrimp. Three minutes for medium shrimp. Four minutes for larger shrimp, and up to five minutes for the jumbos. After boiling for the suggested times, I do, however, recommend that the shrimp sit in the water for four or five minutes, so that they will absorb a little of the salt. I like to cool the water a bit by adding ice, if I've got it handy.

Steamed shrimp can be cooked for about the same length of time, but I really prefer mine boiled in salted water. Some people swear by shrimp that have been steamed over beer, and I'll allow that I have eaten some tasty and juicy shrimp cooked in this manner. Unless you are rigged for steaming, however, you will probably be better off with a very large pot of boiling water. One very handy gadget for boiling shrimp outside are the "fish fryers" that hold several gallons of liquid and are heated by bottled butane gas. Perfect.

Here's what you will need in order to cook the world's best shrimp:

shrimp

water

salt

That's all. No spice. True, I've eaten and enjoyed all manner of spicy shrimp. Spice is fine if you prefer the taste of it to that of shrimp. The people in Louisiana won't like what I'm saying here, and my words might well bring the financial collapse of McCormick and Zatarain, houses that traffic in spices and spice mixes for shrimp, crabs, and the like. I speak not from malice but only in the interest of culinary truth.

Spiced or unspiced, the key to perfectly boiled shrimp is to take them out of the water before they cook too long. This is a matter not only of taste and texture but also of shucking. If shrimp are cooked too long, the meat sticks to the shells, making them difficult to peel at the table.

I prefer a lot of salt in the water, at least ½ cup to a gallon. (If that seems like too much salt, remember that the shrimp will be in their shells and that they will stay in the water for only a short time.) After cooking the shrimp, cool the water a little, or at least remove it from the heat source. Let the shrimp steep for a few minutes in the liquid in order to soak in a little salt. Then take the shrimp up with a strainer quickly and drain them, or pour the water off them.

It's best to start eating the shrimp while they are hot. Merely pile them onto a large platter and put them in the middle of the table. Each guest should have a plate, a cup for sauce, a bowl for shells, a finger bowl with water in it, and a large napkin. The shrimp are peeled right at the table and touched to the sauce before eating. All I want with boiled shrimp is some good hot bread. Or maybe garlic bread.

My good wife normally makes the sauce for the shrimp that we serve, but she won't be pinned down to exact measures, saying that it is best to proceed by taste. Recently I watched her prepare a batch, however, and here's what she used, exactly:

Helen's Sauce

1 cup melted butter
juice of 1 large lemon
1 clove garlic, pressed or minced

Melt the butter and stir in the garlic. Let this steep for an hour or two. Strain out the garlic, then stir in the lemon juice. Let it sit for at least an hour, at room temperature, before serving. It can, however, be made ahead and refrigerated. Serve this sauce in individual bowls, so that each guest will have sauce at hand. The shrimp is first peeled, then held by the tail, and then touched to the sauce before being popped into the mouth. Thus, people who want lots of sauce can dip the shrimp deeper. Those who want more shrimp taste, or who are on a diet, can barely touch the shrimp to the sauce.

Some people want a red sauce for shrimp, and, when we have guests, we will offer both red and butter sauces. Children, especially, like a pretty sauce. Sooner or later, however, all guests will dunk a shrimp into the butter sauce and be converted. The same butter sauce and sauce strategy can be used to great advantage on lobster, stone crabs, other crabs, and crawfish when these good foods are served hot or warm.

If you want to serve chilled shrimp, however, a chilled red sauce is called for. Use your favorite recipe, or try mine:

Red Sauce

1 cup catsup
¼ cup red wine
juice of 1 large lemon
2 cloves garlic
1 teaspoon olive oil
1 teaspoon prepared horseradish
1 teaspoon Dijon mustard
¼ teaspoon Tabasco sauce

Crush or mince the garlic and put it into 1 teaspoon of olive oil for several hours or, better, for overnight. Strain out the garlic and put the garlic oil into a small bowl. Mix in all other ingredients. Chill. Serve cold.

What kind of shrimp should you boil? Fresh ones, the fresher the better. Most true fans buy and boil the shrimp in the shell. Then they are peeled at the table. This is quite easy, as compared to picking crabs or cracking lobsters. Some persnickety people will want to peel and devein the shrimp before cooking them, or before putting them on the table. That's their choice. I normally buy shrimp with the head removed, especially if I have guests of unknown stomach, but the truth is that heads-on shrimp are just as good, if not better, for boiling, provided that they are fresh. Frozen shrimp, in my opinion, should be cooked by some other method—or well spiced.

The size of the shrimp makes a difference, of course, in cooking times and in ease of eating. With large shrimp, you get more meat per peeling, but, even so, I prefer the medium shrimp, at least for boiling. Part of the total experi-

91 |

ence of a shrimp boil is in having to work for what you get. The meal lasts longer, you eat more, and good talk is bound to develop.

How much shrimp should you allow per person? If I am hungry, I can eat a pound (unshucked weight, without heads). Seeing a one-pound pile of shrimp, most people will say they can't possibly eat all of them. But if you'll cook the shrimp right, you aren't likely to have many left over, no matter how many you cook, within reason. Get plenty, and if you have leftovers, fine. Refrigerate them for shrimp salad the next day.

Tiny shrimp, boiled only for a minute or two, are also very good, but peeling them may be too much trouble for guests. You may even expend as much energy peeling the shrimp as you gain by eating the meat. Once I ate such shrimp for 12 hours. I was in the Navy at the time and we had dropped anchor at Guantanamo Bay, Cuba. This was before the revolution. Anyhow, several of us ordered shrimp at a large table in a sidewalk cafe. No doubt seeing a good thing, the restauranteur brought out the smallest shrimp he had. We started on them, along with some good dark beer of some sort. We kept the table going day and night, delighting the Cuban fish mongers, who no doubt unloaded all their tiny shrimp at a premium price. Of course, most of our company left the sidewalk table from time to time to take care of other business or to straighten out a snarl in the Guantanamo traffic. Back then, Cubans drove even worse than the Italians.

In addition to drinking the good dark beer and eating shrimp, we also kept a jukebox hot, playing, over and over, a Spanish language version of "Doggie in the Window." The only Spanish that we understood, however, was the periodic barking of the little doggie. We all thought this was terribly funny, and each series of barks was occasion for another mug of beer and, if needed, another platter or two of tiny shrimp.

The Cuban shrimp eating party started at about 10 in the morning, and went on all day and most of the night. At some time past the 2 a.m. curfew, two members of the U.S. Navy Shore Partol escorted us back to our ship at Guantanamo Bay. But not until we ordered 10 pounds of boiled shrimp to go.

Crabs, lobsters, and crawfish can be boiled by the method set forth above, but of course the cooking times will vary, depending on size. Lobsters are easy, in my opinion, and should be boiled until they turn pink. The time will vary with the size of the lobster, but, with lobsters of normal size, served one lobster per person, you can start looking for the pink after boiling for 15 minutes. Usually, blue crabs should be boiled for about 8 to 10 minutes—12 at the most for very large crabs. Stone crab claws take 12 minutes or longer. Some stone crabs are quite large, and can have several pounds of meat in a single claw. These will require longer cooking. The meat in stone crabs, encased in a thick shell, doesn't seem to dry out as much as some other similar meats, so that longer cooking isn't quite as disastrous.

For all of these shellfish, except freshwater crawfish, I prefer to peel or shuck the tail or claws at the table and touch the meat to the melted butter sauce. (Meat from blue crabs, of course, isn't easy to get off in chunks large enough to dunk; you're on your own here, so just do the best you can.) Freshwater crawfish have a large head and a small tail, without much meat. The tail is somewhat difficult to peel at the table, in my opinion, and is therefore not as suitable as peeled shrimp for home cooking. If you have a couple of burlap bags of crawfish and want to boil them, the best bet is to cook the whole thing and set them on the table very hot. Boil for 2 to 4 minutes, depending on size. Cooking them longer will make them much more difficult to peel.

When you're ready to eat, pick up a crawfish with your

fingers on each end. Break it in half, then suck from the middle. This gets the meat out of the tail and some "sauce" from the head part. At least, that's the way the Cajuns say to do it. Maybe this method makes a good show for the tourists, but I suspect that most Cajuns eat their crawfish in an etouffée, at least when nobody is looking.

DUST OFF THE CROCKPOT

Newlyweds who fail to catch a large fish on day two of their honeymoon may be in for domestic trouble on down the road. To insure happiness and ward off evil, the couple must step over a large fish the day after their wedding, according to an old custom in Tunisia. If either of the twain happens to be an American hunter or lean-meat fanatic, then more powerful magic may be required.

Maybe I'm bucking the fast-food trend, but I recommend an old fashioned crockpot for a wedding gift, not a hi-tech microwave. It's true that microwave ovens, by some electronic sleight of hand, zap out meat dinners quicker than the working cook can say "shish kebab skewer." No mess. Maybe no fuss. But the modern divorce rate indicates that something is missing. Taste? Color? Texture? Maybe. The sizzle of the skillet or the barbecue grill? Maybe. Something more? Yes. Something sensuous. The palate is vitalized by a sense of smell, and a pervading aroma requires time to accumulate. For that reason, the slow-cooking electric crockpot makes a home-steeping magic that can't be matched by the microwave oven.

Career persons, chefs, and workaday epicures take note: The crockpot can be loaded and turned on in the morning *before* leaving the house instead of after the return at night. (Don't worry. The crockpot was designed to cook unattended all day long without scorching or burning the food. It cooks on low, steady heat from electrical elements in the side of the pot. It has no hotspots, and on low setting it does not boil.) Knowing that a good meal simmers at home will add pleasant expectation to the day. Like the radiant warmth from an open hearth fire, the aroma from the crockpot welcomes one home from the windy road, the work place, or the cold duck blind.

It's true that few modern people want to deal with a long list of ingredients early in the morning. Fortunately, the crockpot recipe doesn't have to be complicated or long. Try this:

5-pound roast, lean and trimmed of fat

1 clove garlic

½ cup black breakfast coffee

black pepper

Trim the roast and cut a narrow slit into the meat. Peel the garlic and insert it into the slit. Sprinkle the roast with pepper and fit it into the crockpot. Pour the coffee over the meat, cover with the lid, and cook on low heat for 9 hours. Use the pot liquid as gravy.

If you want a full meal, add some onions, carrots, and potatoes along with the meat, as in the recipe below.

One-Pot Dinner

3- to 4-pound roast

3 medium potatoes

2 medium onions

2 carrots

1 stalk celery

1 clove garlic

½ cup water

salt and pepper

With a thin, sharp knife, make two well-spaced slits in the roast. Peel the garlic clove, cut it in half lengthwise, and insert a piece into either slit. Sprinkle the roast lightly with salt and pepper. Peel or scrape the vegetables. Quarter the potatoes and onions; slice the celery and carrots crossways. Put the vegetables into the crockpot. Then fit the roast on top of the vegetables. Pour in ½ cup of water, cover, and turn on low. Let cook for 10 to 12 hours.

Crockpot Goulash

I must have tried a hundred recipes for goulash of one kind or another. Here is one of my favorites, which I designed especially for the crockpot.

Filling the Pot

3 pounds lean beef, cubed

1 pound fresh pork, cubed

12 to 18 ounces fresh mushrooms

3 cups chopped onions

1 large can tomato paste (12-ounce size)

1½ cups red wine

2 teaspoons salt

1 teaspoon black pepper

Late Editions

1 cup sour cream

1 tablespoon sweet Hungarian paprika

Coarsely chop the onions and put them into the bottom of the pot. Add the meat, tomato paste, wine, salt, and pepper. Wash the mushrooms and place them on top of the meat mixture. Fill all the way to the top, even making a mound to fit under the dome-shaped lid. If the pot won't hold all the mushrooms, save what's left and add them in about 2 hours, after the ingredients cook down a bit. Cook on low for 10 hours or so. About 30 minutes before time to eat, turn the heat to high and stir in the sour cream and paprika. This goulash goes good with rice, a hearty green salad, and vegetables of your choice. If you are a gravy fan, have plenty of good bread. Serves 8 to 10. Leftovers can be frozen.

Note: I use whole mushrooms for this dish, preferably from 1 to 1½ inches in diameter. This practice delights people who love mushrooms, while allowing others either to push them aside easily or to avoid them when filling the plate directly from the crockpot.

Jalapeño Roast

If you like the flavor of jalapeño peppers, be sure to try this recipe. I always leave the peppers whole so that they can be omitted from one's serving if they aren't wanted.

> *4-pound beef roast*
> *4 to 6 fresh jalapeño peppers*
> *1 can stewed tomatoes (14½-ounce size)*
> *½ cup water*
> *salt*

Sprinkle the roast with salt. Put it into the crockpot, then add water, tomatoes, and jalapeño peppers. Turn crockpot to low and cook for 11 or 12 hours. Serves 8 to 10.

Leftovers: Refrigerate leftover roast and gravy. The next day, chop roast up into gravy and heat. Serve over cooked rice.

Crockpot Chili

This recipe makes a chili with distinctive flavor and texture. It calls for both ground and cubed meat, which can be from beef as well as elk or moose. If you try it with fatty beef (or bear) instead of lean meat, omit the sausage and add ½ teaspoon of sage.

> *2½ pounds lean red meat, cut into 1-inch cubes*
> *1½ pounds lean red meat, ground*
> *¼ pound whole-hog pork sausage*
> *1 can (6-ounce size) tomato paste*
> *2 tomato paste cans of water (or 2 cups)*
> *1 tablespoon dark molasses*
> *1 tablespoon salt*
> *½ tablespoon black pepper*
> *2 tablespoons ground cumin*
> *5 tablespoons chili powder*
> *1 or more pods of hot pepper of calculated potency*
> *1 medium onion, diced*
> *3 cloves garlic, minced*
> *cornmeal mush (optional)*
> *2 cups chopped onions, chilled (optional)*
> *grated cheese (optional)*
> *sour cream (optional)*

Put tomato sauce and two cans of water into the crockpot. Stir in molasses, pepper, salt, cumin, chili powder, onions, and garlic. Add a pod or two of your favorite hot pepper, if you know its strength. Add meats and mix. Cover tightly and put on low heat for 10 hours. Serve with crackers.

For an interesting variation, top chili bowls with chopped onions. This dish works best if the chopped onions are quite cold, contrasting with the hot chili. Also, grated cheese can be used for a topping, with or without the onions. And try a dollop of sour cream atop each serving of chili. Put the chilled onions (on ice), the sour cream, and the grated cheese on the table in separate bowls so that your guests can experiment.

Toppings work best with a thick chili, and I like to thicken mine with a mush made of white corn meal that has been ground as fine as flour. Put ¼ cup of cornmeal into a bowl and stir in a little water until a mush is made. Turn crockpot to high, then stir the mixture into the chili, one spoonful at the time, testing for consistency as you go.

Dijon Pork Roast

I normally cook this recipe with Dijon mustard, but any sort of prepared mustard will do. If you've got some good brown creole mustard, be sure to try it. I've used this basic recipe for several meats, including venison, but my favorite is fresh pork. Boston butts, picnics, and other cuts of suitable size are fine. *Warning*: Fresh pork cooked by this method tastes so good, and smells so good, that people on a diet should not be tempted to taste it.

1 pork roast, 4 or 5 pounds
3 tablespoons Dijon or other prepared mustard

3 tablespoons dark brown sugar
¼ cup apple juice
salt and pepper

Wash the roast, pat it dry, and sprinkle all sides with salt and pepper. Mix the mustard and the brown sugar, then coat the roast with the mixture. Put ¼ cup apple juice into the crockpot, then fit the roast in. Turn to high heat for four hours. Turn to low for an hour or two. Remove the roast from the crockpot and put it onto a serving platter.

If you have used fatty fresh pork, discard the liquid in the crockpot. If you've used beef or venison, consider the gravy. Thicken it with flour or corn starch and serve over rice or mashed potatoes.

Variation: Sage is often used with pork, and is especially good with fresh pork. Try 1 tablespoon powdered sage mixed in with the mustard and brown sugar.

Turkish Fish Soup à la Timucuan

I came about this dish in a curious manner. While living on Timucuan Island in Florida's Lake Weir, I often caught and dressed out large numbers of bluegill. (The fish and game department encouraged anglers to keep bluegills in order to prevent overpopulation, and, with the support of my family and friends, I did my best to keep Lake Weir in ecological balance.) One day I came in after sundown and didn't dress the fish until after dark. When I started down to the beach to throw the fish heads "to the turtles," I shined my flashlight along the water's edge. There must have been 15 alligators lined up on the white sands of my patio beach, all pointed toward the house, waiting, I suppose for fish heads. It looked like footage from a Tarzan movie. I took the bucket of heads back inside, locked the sliding glass door, drew the curtain, and told my children to stay put. (Never again did I throw fish heads into the lake, and soon the alligators quit lining up on my beach.)

So . . . I had a bucketful of bluegill heads and didn't want to throw them into the lake. Nor did I want to put them into the garbage can outside because of the raccoons. I thought about burying the heads beside our orange tree, but the spade was in a little utility shed down by the beach (i.e., right beside the alligators). The only thing I could do, I figured, was put the fish heads into an empty milk container and freeze them. I did this on the sly while my good wife was talking over the telephone.

A few weeks later, we had guests coming out for a fish supper and she got out four jugs of frozen fish to thaw. Of course, she got out the fish heads. When she discovered what she had done, she blamed *me* for her mistake.

"Well, don't worry," I said, quite worried myself. "What we've got here is three jugs of fish for frying and enough makings for *Shorbet el Samak*," which was the name of a fish soup that I had recently read about in *A Book of Middle Eastern Food* by Claudia Roden. (It was from this text that I learned the Tunisian custom of stepping over large fish the day after the wedding.) I need not have worried. The soup was truly delicious! I've cooked it a number of times since then, and the crockpot version below is my favorite.

The Stock

fish heads, bones, and tails
4 tablespoons wine vinegar
2 large onions

2 tablespoons finely chopped parsley
3 cloves garlic, crushed
salt and pepper
1 teaspoon turmeric

Late Additions

1 pound boneless fish fillets or fingers
1 tablespoon butter
yolks of 3 medium chicken eggs
juice of 1 large lemon
ground cinnamon

Pour 1 quart of water and a cup of vinegar into the crockpot and turn on low heat. Add salt, pepper, and turmeric. Spread a piece of well-rinsed cheesecloth of suitable size (about 2 feet on each side) onto a table or countertop and pile the fish bones, heads, onions, garlic, and parsley in the middle. Pull in the corners of the cheesecloth, twist, and tie, thereby making a bag to hold the ingredients. (Of course, the dish can be cooked without the cheesecloth, but the liquid will have to be poured from the crockpot, strained, and added back.) Put the cheesecloth bag into the pot, cover tightly, turn the heat to low, and cook for about 8 hours.

Lift out the cheesecloth bag, allowing it to drain into the crockpot, and dispose of it as prudently as you can. (Alligators, by the way, don't care much for the flavor of turmeric.) Turn the crockpot to high and stir a tablespoon of butter into the broth. Add a quart of *boiling* water. (If you use cold water, you'll have to wait for the slow crockpot to heat it up.) Add fish fillets. Let poach for 20 minutes, or less for thin fillets such as those from small flounder.

While the fish is poaching, beat three chicken egg yolks and put them into a bowl. Whisk in the lemon juice. Stir in half a cup of stock from the crockpot. Add this mixture to the crockpot, turn to high, and heat almost to boiling. But do not let boil—unless you want curdled Turkish soup. Stir well but make sure that the fish holds together in good-sized chunks. (If you've got very flaky fish, you may need to remove the fillets before stirring in the egg yolk mixture.)

With a spatula, put the fish pieces into serving bowls and ladle the soup over it. Sprinkle lightly with cinnamon. Taste the soup, praise Allah, uncork a bottle of wine, and break open a loaf of good French bread.

BE IT HEAVEN OR HELL?

Most anglers and commercial fishermen know that they can catch a better fish than they can raise. For eating purposes, pellet-fed catfish or rainbow trout are simply not as tasty as wild fish. Yet, public relations writers and advertising sharps employed by the catfish farms and the aquaculture industry would have us believe otherwise. The misconception is spreading fast, even among those anglers who actually practice the catch-and-release ethic. Already aquaculture propaganda has filtered down to popular cookbooks, articles, and TV shows.

Anglers worthy of the name won't have much trouble finding and catching good fare, but it is becoming more and more difficult to find river-run catfish in markets and supermarkets. Fortunately, there are still a few eating houses, often at the water's edge, that specialize in wild catfish. Usually these establishments are nothing fancy, but they do serve up all that a good man can eat at a fair price. True catfish connoisseurs will travel for some distance overland to such places.

Once, for example, I attended a meeting in Tallahassee, Florida, between the late Lew Childre, Jim Bagley, and some other big wheels of the fishing tackle trade. The occasion called for fried catfish. But one among us said that he would die and go to hell before he would eat pond-raised cats. He was mad at a wordman who had said, while making a little nasty face on public television, that commercially raised catfish don't taste muddy like their wild river cousins. Everyone at our meeting agreed that wordman Walter Cronkite wouldn't have said it.

Anyhow, the conversation whetted our appetite for cat-fish, and Childre claimed to know of a place that still served up river cats. It lay somewhere between us and Wewahitcha. Out of Tallahassee and toward the big river we came, hungry and hellbent for Miss Emma's Forked Tail Cafe. Bagley drove the lead car, and, under the handle Baitman, he soon made CB contact with Birddog, a truck driver who pinpointed the location and confirmed that the cafe did indeed serve up river-run catfish. Ten-four, and full speed ahead.

The cafe lived up to our expectations, especially after we filled the place up with good company and good talk about tackle and angling and prime fish. During the repast, how-ever, Jim Bagley kept glancing at me over the platters of golden-fried, 10-inch-long forked-tail catfish, as if trying to figure out what I was doing there. I didn't know either. Childre had introduced me as *his* wordman, which sounded too much like a CB handle for complete comfort. Comfortable or not, however, I ate more than my share of the perfectly cooked catfish.

Later, I found out that Childre was determined to hire me to write news releases, advertisements, and such for his tackle manufacturing and promotion firm. All night long he talked to me, head to head, revealing what amounted to a highly personal religion—with a catfish connection. Lew believed himself to be God's man on this good earth for the fishing pole. The rod, he said, is nothing but a fishing pole with guides on it, and the baitcasting reel fits right into the scheme of things. And he needed *me* to help spread the Word. Of course, I was torn between being flattered and flabbergasted. Finally, I had to tell him flat out that I really wasn't looking for a job, and that I wouldn't be a good wordman anyhow.

"I know you've got your own plans, A.D.," Lew said, "writing articles and books and such. But maybe you need to change directions. Look, it's like flying an airplane into the backcountry to go fishing. You find the river all right and come in for what looks like a smooth landing. But at the last minute you see snags sticking up out of the water, and you swerve a little and land in a big slough that opens up under the treetops." As he spoke, he wielded an imaginary steering wheel, then, with the palm of his hand, he set the airplane down smoothly. "That's where the big fish are anyhow."

"Well that's all fine and dandy, Lew," I said, "if you're driving the airplane. But it's rough on passengers who, like me, are just along for the ride."

Lew didn't laugh. "Is that your answer, then?" he asked, a little put out now.

"Yes," I said.

For a long while we sat in silence. Finally, just at the crack of dawn, Lew stood up, looked down on me, and said, "You're just hard-headed, A.D. But so be it. I've warned you. You know that Lew has told you. When you get up there——" He paused for effect and pointed straight up. "When you get up there before the Man, what are you going to say? You know that He knows that Lew has told you. You can't deny it, A.D. It's too late to deny it now. You're standing before His throne on a flat white cloud. On your left is a black hole. You don't know what's at the bottom of it. At a table on your right sit me, Jim Bagley, Walter Cronkite, Shag Shahid, and some others—eating catfish. We stop and look at you. We all want you to come and join our company and eat some hush puppies and catfish with us instead of going to that other place. But we can't help you now. It's up to you. What are you going to say, A.D.?"

I thought on the matter for a long while in silence. Lew Childre had, I knew, done more to improve baitcasting rods and reels than any man of our time. Modern bass fishing would not be the same without him. Now he wanted to venture into spinning, spincasting, fly fishing, surf casting, etc.—and he was inviting me to be a part of it. A part of it all.

"The choice is yours," Lew said.

"Are they river-run cats?" I asked.

Epilogue

After I wrote the above piece, Lew was killed in an airplane crash and the Childre line of rods and reels has been taken over by Browning in Utah. I think of Lew often, and I like to believe that somehow he gets wind of it whenever I work in a choice word or two in praise of quality fishing tackle and good river catfish. In any case, I would like to beseech you, Gentle Reader, to consider Lew's singular vision of Heaven or Hell—and decide where you want to go.

PART 2

A Few Vegetables

After completing the first draft of this section, I worried that my choice of vegetables might smack too much of Southern cooking and soul food. After thinking on the matter for some time, I decided not to take a stand or to defend my choice. I merely want to point out that the vegetables and recipes that I cover herein are, for the most part, *American* food. The American Indians cultivated and relished beans, potatoes, squash, corn, and tomatoes, all of which, along with peanuts and chili peppers, were unknown on the continents of Europe or Africa before Columbus ventured forth and traffic began.

HOW TO COOK SQUASH

According to Joel Vance, a flying zucchini hit a game warden's vehicle in the state of Missouri. It seems that a woman, headed south, stopped her car to pick up what turned out to be a large zucchini in the middle of the road. After she had put it on the seat by her side and had gained speed again, she apparently realized that the thing wasn't a watermelon. Quickly she threw it out the window—just as the game warden's vehicle came around a bend in the road. Of course, a large zucchini going south at 55 miles an hour can do considerable damage to a motor vehicle heading north at 55!

Back in his office, the game warden was required to fill out a formal damage estimate and report, which, of course, had a line for "Cause of Accident." I don't know how he explained what had taken place, or whether he had retained the zucchini for evidence. My own guess is that he didn't falsify the record because he couldn't explain the incident convincingly in writing. He did it because he couldn't spell *zucchini* in such a way that it seemed natural. Look at it. Zucchini. That's right. Z-u-c-c-h-i-n-i. Look it up. There *is* no really good way to spell the word, just as there is no really good way to cook the things.

But I consider myself to be an adventurous sort when it comes to culinary matters, and I've eaten the zucchini in a number of different ways, modes, and configurations—cooked, raw, and half-done—but I've never eaten the same recipe more than once, except possibly for my mother's casserole that contained a little zucchini. The reason for multitudinous zucchini recipes, of course, is that people keep looking for ways to make this green gourd taste better than merely edible. I understand that somebody actually wrote a whole book on how to cook zucchini. I rest my case on the grounds that if anyone had discovered a good way to cook the things, a whole book on the subject simply would not have been needed. I also found it noteworthy that Bert Greene in *Greene on Greens* had one chapter on squash and another on zucchini. Separate things. But strangely ubiquitous. I even found a zucchini recipe in *The Africa News Cookbook*. But the recipe came from Chad, and the authors, or some astute editor, noted that the zucchini was probably due to the French influence in Chad. I don't doubt that a bit.

There are other squash-like vegetables, such as the acorn squash and the chayote, that are edible. I don't pretend to fully understand all of the squash terms—and I'm not sure that I want to. I've eaten most of these squash, as well as pumpkins, at one time or another, and I've found them all to be tolerable. (Remember, I never said that zucchini isn't tolerable; to be sure, I'll take a bite or two any day when I'm really hungry.) For the very best eating, however, forget all these culinary off-shoots and find yourself some ordinary crooked-neck yellow squash. But pick them while they are quite small, preferably just after the bloom has dropped off the end and before the "goose neck" has developed—and before the seeds take shape and the outer skin grows bumpy and hard. If you have to peel and remove seed from squash, they are too old to eat, although the seeds might be tasty if they are properly dried and toasted. Size isn't always a reliable guide, but usually the best squash will be no more than 4 inches in length.

Warning: if you follow my way with these small squash, you're going to need lots of 'em. My recipe and cooking technique reduces them to only a fraction of their original volume, and they are so good that your guests are going to demand several big helpings. What you end up with is a concentration of squash flavor instead of watery pulp. When

prepared by my method, squash can provide an eating experience like no other. Here's what you need:

half a gallon of young squash
2 medium onions
half a pound of cured bacon
salt and pepper

Get a cast-iron Dutch oven suitable for stovetop cooking.
Fry the bacon in it. Remove bacon, crumble, and set aside.
Peel the onions, dice them, and sauté them in the bacon
drippings. Pour off about half the bacon drippings. Wash
the young squash. Cut the ends off and discard. Slice the
squash crossways about ½-inch thick and pile the wheels
into the Dutch oven atop the onions. If the container won't
hold all the squash, let a batch cook down a bit, then add
the rest.

After you put all the squash into the pot, cover them and
reduce the heat to low. Stirring from time to time, simmer
and steam until the squash are very, very tender and can be
mashed easily with a spoon or fork. Remove the lid, salt
and pepper to taste, and continue to cook, stirring and
mashing often so that the bottom won't burn. (Note carefully that this process, toward the end, is a full time job and
requires all of your attention—unless you want scorched
squash.) The idea, of course, is to cook most of the
moisture out of the squash, concentrating the flavor. When
this has been done correctly, the squash will be slightly
brown and, I admit, a little greasy. Stir in the crumbled
bacon and serve immediately.

Variations: Some folks prefer to cook squash with salt
pork instead of cured bacon. Salt pork is fine and fitting—
as long as you use only the yellow crooked-necked squash
in the recipe.

Warning: Don't be tempted to use up a green zucchini

in the above yellow squash recipe. But don't throw it out on the highway, either, where it might be hazardous to traffic. Hold on to it in case you get warts. According to Bert Greene, the old English people believed that you could remove warts by touching them with the cut end of a zucchini during a full moon, and then burying the zucchini in a field that faces north. Try it.

COLLARD GREENS AND CORNDODGERS

Cookbooks seem to be costing more and more these days for less and less, but I reasoned that any work whose title contained the words "uncommon vegetables" would be worth a considerable sum. Paying dearly, I purchased such a book by mail. Eagerly I unboxed it at the Post Office, and eagerly I opened it at random. I was quite astounded, somewhat disappointed, and no little bit irritated when the pages parted to a chapter heading and text about collards. That's right. *Collards.* Collard greens. Uncommon vegetables? Good Lord. It was lucky for me that none of the local people were looking over my shoulder. I would have been the laughing stock of our town and country, where collards are as common as gully dirt.

The people hereabouts had already been eyeing me rather curiously ever since I announced in our cafe, on the town square, that kudzu and purslane are edible. But the idea of a collard sandwich didn't come from me, or from the new book on uncommon vegetables. To that I'll swear. What happened is as follows: a fellow named Harpe Chancey, who for a number of years operated a service station across the square, went into the cafe every morning at five minutes past six. Every morning he asked for a collard sandwich, knowing, of course, that such an item wasn't on the breakfast menu. The joke got rather stale after 12 or 13 years.

On a crisp morning in the fall of the year, at first frost—which is a good time for collards—the owner of the restaurant stood ready by the cash register. He watched the clock. He watched the street. At five minutes past six, as usual, Harpe parked his two-toned pick-up truck out front as usual, came in, hung his hat on the tree, and took his regular seat at the large community table, saying, as usual, "I'll take a collard sandwich." He didn't ask why so many of the town's people had gathered in the cafe so early in the morning.

"How's that?" the cafe owner asked, putting his hand to his ear as though he were hard of hearing. He had to strain a little to accomplish this, since his neck was in a white plaster cast.

Harpe looked around at the crowd, grinned, and said, "Whoo-o-o it's cold out there. Has everybody been possum hunting all night?" He liked to joke around with the towns-people, and possum hunting was one of his standard topics, right up there with collard sandwiches.

"We're out of possum," the cafe owner said, not cracking a smile.

"I didn't *order* any possum," Harpe said, acting a little huffy now. "I said I want a collard sandwich. Are you hard of hearing, you broke-neck rascal?"

With only a hint of a smile, the restauranteur dapperly touched the bright yellow pencil to his tongue, then wrote on his hand-sized order pad. Once the documentation was in order, he said, "One collard sandwich. Anything else?"

Snickers came from the crowd, and Harpe began to suspect something was afoot.

"You better not bring me no collard sandwich," he whispered.

"One collard sandwich coming up," the owner said, loudly, wheeling and heading for the kitchen. Quickly he came back with a cold collard sandwich squared up perfectly on a white blue-rimmed plate. Greenish juice oozed out the sides of the sandwich and puddled in the plate. Harpe paled and claimed that he was just joking and that | *118*

he only wanted some coffee like he always got and . . . and
. . . and he wasn't about to eat a cold collard sandwich. Not
for breakfast anyway. And certainly not in front of all those
people.

"Yes, hell, you are going to eat it," the restauranteur said.
He nodded toward the open doorway to the kitchen. Out
came a huge chef. He stood at the head of the table, between Harpe and the front door, and crossed his arms, with
a meat clever in each hand. (He was, we found out later, a
down-and-out wrestler who had been hired for the job, at
least until the cafe owner's broken neck got well.)

Silence fell over the place. Nobody at the tables stirred
coffee. Nobody rattled knives and forks. All eyes were on
Harpe.

"Well," he said, "I reckon I asked for a collard sandwich.
Pass me a little of that pepper sauce to go with it."

Indeed, pepper sauce with collards is something of a tra-
dition, at least in some parts of the country, and opinions
are firm on exactly how hot the sauce must be. We'll get to
pepper sauce a little later.

Harpe and other folks hereabouts plant collards in late
summer or early fall. The plants grow fast, making a stalk
about 3 feet high at maturity. Thus, a few stalks of collards
can feed lots of folks. The large leaves are picked from the
stalk—bottom leaf first, always. This eventually makes the
collard plant look like a miniature palm tree, and rows of
such stalks are easily seen from the roadway as one drives
around our community. Collards are hardy plants that can
withstand more cold weather than most other greens. Thus,
they are often eaten all the winter long—and on into the
spring, at least in the more temperate zones. Families have
broken up and neighbors have had fist fights concerning
whether the best collards are picked off young stalks or
whether they get sweeter after the first frost falls.

When the collard greens have been picked and washed,

it's best to cut the stem out of the large leaves. (But I have eaten them with the stems left in, and I have no real objection to this, provided that they are well chopped.) Some people cut the leaves up before boiling the greens, and others wait until they are cooked. I'm not hard to please, so either way is fine with me.

A lot of people who favor bland foods will boil or blanch collards in a first water, then drain them and cook them until tender in new water. I prefer only one boiling, but on the other hand I like a lot of taste to my greens.

There are apparently many recipes for cooking collards, and the "uncommon vegetable" book had quite a few, including one that was an "adaptation" of a "Southern Classic." Well, adapted to *what*? Why fool around with a classic? I'll tell you why. Because those cookbook writers in New York, San Francisco, and New Orleans can't let a classic recipe stand. They have to add stuff to it so that they can't be accused of stealing the recipe. Each year, the recipes and lists of ingredients grow longer and longer. Anyhow, here is what I consider to be the basic recipe for self-respecting collard eaters:

Collards

3 to 5 pounds of fresh greens
½ pound salt pork
water

Corndodgers

2 cups fine white corn meal, water-ground style
1 teaspoon salt

½ teaspoon black pepper
¾ cup of water (more or less)

Put the salt pork into a large pot and add a little water. Cover and cook it for an hour. Cut up the meat. Add the collard leaves and let them settle. Add enough water to almost cover the greens. Bring to a quick boil, cover, and simmer for an hour.

To make the corndodgers while the collards are cooking, mix the meal, salt, and pepper with warm water. Let the mixture sit for 15 minutes, then consider the texture. Add a little more water, if you must. Shape the meal mixture into patties or bite-size dollops.

After the collard greens have cooked for an hour, chop the leaves with a knife and fork. Add corndodgers and simmer for 20 mintues. Transfer collards and corndodgers to a serving bowl and break out a bottle of pepper sauce. But save some of the corndodgers for the potlicker—which is, to me, even better and more nutritious than the greens.

I might add that the Greeks and the Romans believed collards to have curative powers, and the great Julius Caesar is said to have eaten collards after a feast to head off indigestion. What Caesar ate, in my opinion, was collard green potlicker. If he could only have tried cornpone with it, he would have mustered his legions and set sail for the corn fields of Mexico instead of fooling away his days on the Nile with Cleopatra.

Anyhow, you've now got the world's best ungarnished recipe for collard greens. Much disagreement crops up, of course, on this point or that. The corndodgers are also subject to debate. Many people say that the meal mixture should be rolled out into a log, then cut into slices. Others shape them by hand. A lot of folks make corndodgers by a tolerable way—but then turn right around and call them dumplings. (Dumplings, I say, are made with flour and go well in ham pie or chicken pie or blackbird pie.) But note this: That fancy book on uncommon vegetables specified *flour* dumplings in the collard recipe. Flour dumplings in collard greens? Can you imagine that? I can't either.

In any case, make sure that leftover collards are warmed up before serving them to guests or family. I have it on good authority that cold collards are difficult to swallow—especially in soggy sandwiches.

The pepper sauce mentioned above is not the commercial "pepper sauce," such as Tabasco or the reddish "Louisiana hot sauce." It is made by putting small hot chili pepper pods into a jar, then covering them with vinegar. (The sauce is made from fresh pods, not dried pods, which add a flavor in addition to the hotness.) The vinegar and pepper pods sit for at least a month, and the resulting liquid is poured over greens, or eaten with oysters. A local fellow of my acquaintance makes a *five* gallon jug of this stuff every year.

Apparently one hot pepper may not be as good as another, and I know of a couple who survived a good deal of domestic trouble' over pepper sauce. Now they grow two kinds of hot peppers each year, and they make two separate batches of pepper sauce for their table. His and hers. If you want to make some pepper sauce, try my wife's grandfather's recipe:

Raley Anderson's Pepper Sauce

chiltipiquins
apple cider vinegar
salt

Pick some peppers fresh from the stalk or buy some fresh peppers at the market. Find some small jars with a small mouth. Ideally, the mouth should be just large enough to push a pepper through. (The idea, of course, is that the pepper sauce can be served directly simply by shaking the jar over your food.) Fill the jar with peppers. Cover the peppers with apple cider vinegar, into which a little salt has been dissolved. Let the jars sit for a month or longer before using.

Warning: the peppers used in this sauce can be quite hot. Never eat one without first breaking it open and tasting it with a quick flick of the tongue. Pot a whole one into your mouth and bite into it at your own considerable risk.

Variation: I have also made the pepper sauce with green jalapeño peppers and 1 clove of peeled garlic, covered with apple cider vinegar. It's very good, and I also eat the pickled jalapeño peppers or use them in chili or other hot dishes.

Pepper sauce is also commonly used on turnip greens, but, alas, too many people are familiar only with the turnip roots. In any case, the best eating might well come with a combination of greens and roots. This dish is usually prepared with a "bunch" of turnips, containing both leaves and roots. But the leaves on a mature root are a little too old for good eating, and I would therefore like to call attention to my mother's way of handling this problem.

She raised one patch of turnips for the roots, and she raised another patch for the greens. The root turnips were allowed to mature, at which time the roots were harvested and the greens were thrown away. A younger patch of turnip greens, often containing half mustard greens, was sowed and "cut" when the greens were about the size of a silver dollar. These are very tender, and make very, very good eating. My mother actually cut such greens with large scissors. I myself have raised turnips in this manner, and I highly recommend the practice.

I usually plant these in September. A crop can also be grown in the spring, but the season is short because they tend to "head" quickly in hot weather. When getting ready to plant a patch of turnips, clear off a spot of garden or flower bed. Mix a pack of turnip seeds and a pack of mustard seeds in with some sand. Scatter the seeds over the bed by broadcasting them with your hand. Rake the ground a little with a garden rake, which will cover some of the seeds enough for sprouting purposes. In a couple of weeks, you will have a thick stand of leaves. Cut these with scissors, wash, and cook. After this cutting, the leaves will grow out again, and again, until frost kills the plants. Try it. Then cook Miss Bea's recipe:

Miss Bea's Turnips

turnip greens, young and small
turnip roots, mature
pork neck bone
salt
water

Boil the roots until tender. Set aside to cool. Later, peel and dice the roots. Wash the young greens and put them into a pot of suitable size. Add some water, salt, and neck bone. Bring to boil, reduce heat, cover, and simmer until very tender, about 30 minutes. With two long knives, cut the turnip greens several times. Add diced roots and simmer a few minutes. Strain, being sure to save the potlicker and the neck bone. Put the roots and greens onto a platter and garnish with sliced boiled eggs. Have a jar of pepper sauce at hand for those who want it. Serve with pork or other good meat.

| *124*

I am fond of eating the potlicker and the neckbone, although these are not always served at the more formal dinners. Save them for later.

Although my mother usually cooked the above dish with about half turnip greens and half mustard greens, she didn't hesitate to add in a few radish tops or beet tops as well as various wild greens, such as polk or dock or chickory or dandelion.

Personally, I am especially fond of wild mustard, and at least half a dozen varieties of mustard are free for the picking. All make excellent eating. Look for wild mustard at the edge of fields, pastures, and other clearings. Even vacant lots in cities and towns can be productive—and many people who cultivate their own garden weed out wild mustard from time to time. When you find mustard, as often as not there will be lots of it nearby, so that a mess can be gathered in short order. You don't have to pull up the plants. Break off the leaves, or cut them with a knife. A pair of large scissors also works.

For the best eating, pick only the very young, tender leaves. These can be used along with lettuce and other greens in a tossed salad, or they can be boiled in a little salted water and served up like ordinary turnip greens or spinach. Sliced boiled eggs often accompany greens, and some people insist on having a good vinegar-based pepper sauce, as with collards.

The older mustard leaves can also be eaten, but they are tougher and stronger of flavor, often with a somewhat bitter taste. Seasoned epicures may relish the taste, but beginners would be well advised to boil the older mustard leaves for a few minutes, then drain and change the water. Boil the leaves again, along with a little backbone, salt pork, or other seasoning meat, until they are tender. This usually takes 30 minutes or longer, although some people prefer them cooked for only 10 or 15 minutes. Others simmer the greens for an hour or longer. Suit yourself. Before serving, cut the leaves by using a fork and a sharp, thin fillet knife, or by crisscrossing with two knife blades.

Wild mustard greens are quite nutritious, being especially high in vitamins A, B_1, B_2, and C. Of course, any vegetable that is boiled loses some minerals and vitamins to the water. That's reason enough for eating the potlicker. Ladel the liquid into bowls and eat it with soup spoons. Many Southerners will want to break up some cornpone into the liquid, or perhaps cook some corn meal dumplings or corndodgers in the pot along with the liquid, as discussed earlier in this chapter.

Don't consider mustard greens to be a regional dish. Wild mustard grows just about everywhere. And remember that spring isn't the only season for cutting the mustard. On into the summer, the yellow flowered tops of wild mustard greens can be seen for some distance across the field or pasture. The buds of the flowers can also be eaten, like tiny broccoli. (In fact, broccoli is of the mustard family.) But don't boil the buds very long. Usually, two or three minutes will do. Then season them with a little butter, salt, and pepper. I've also eaten immature seed pods in with the buds, and with various Chinese dishes.

Later on, harvest the seeds. It's best to get the whole seed stalks, dry them in the sun for a week, and then frail them over a large bucket or sheet. Winnow the seeds on a windy day. The seeds can be sprinkled over salads, or they can be ground into a powder. To make some outstanding mustard sauce, brown some flour in the oven. Then mix equal parts of browned flour and powdered mustard seeds. Stir in a mixture of half water and half vinegar until you get a sauce that spreads just right. Stir in a little salt and you've got mustard sauce. Other spices and herbs, such as horseradish, can be added. Also, the strength of the mustard sauce can be changed considerably by altering the ratio of flour to mustard powder.

Remember also that growing seasons in some areas of the country are often mild, and one can sometimes find wild mustard with leaves of very good quality until late in the year. December greens are not unheard of. So, cut your mustard whenever you find it. And wherever.

Perhaps I should add that I have enjoyed roots of turnips and rutabagas cooked in various ways, and in such dishes as Irish stew. Here's one of my favorites:

Suwannee River Turnip Roots

I really don't know where this recipe originated, but I came upon it in the Suwannee River area of Florida. It should convince anyone who tries it that there's more than one way to cook a turnip root.

turnip roots

cooking oil

flour

salt

pepper

Peel the turnip roots and slice them about ¼-inch thick. Sprinkle the slices with salt and pepper. Put a little cooking oil into a frying pan over medium heat. Shake the salted turnip slices in a bag with flour. When the oil is hot, fry the turnip slices until they are brown on both sides.

Also try the turnip roots cut like French fries and cooked without flour or batter. If you want to get fancy, sprinkle them with a little paprika before serving.

PEAS AND BEANS

True, I *am* a Southerner. But I refuse to take the rap for dried black-eyed peas. Any food critic or culinary snob who has never feasted on fresh peas that have been properly seasoned and correctly cooked simply doesn't know what it's all about. If picked off the vine and cooked when fresh, blackeyed peas can be very, very good, especially if they are seasoned with a ham hock or two. They are in fact one of my favorite kinds of pea, along with the crowder, partly because they leave a rich, dark potlicker that can be sopped with bread. But most people don't eat blackeyed peas in this manner, and never get them when they are fresh from the vine.

Dried blackeyed peas are what many people eat on New Year's Day. I hate to seem unpatriotic, and I certainly don't want to flout Lady Luck, but I have to admit that I never acquired a taste for them. My mother, a DuPree before she married into the Livingston family, simply didn't cook them at our home during my formative years. She said that she ate so many during the Great Depression that she never wanted another one on her table. I'm sure that there is some truth in what she said, but I think the thing might go deeper into the DuPree lineage.

In any case, most other kinds of dried beans and peas don't appeal to me either, and I really dislike those dried lima beans, especially if they are as large as a 25-cent piece. (I think I was served up too many dried jumbo lima beans during a hitch in the navy, and if there is a good way to cook these things in large batches, the Navy had not found it at that time.) Of course I do eat dried peas and beans occasionally, especially in chili and other dishes, but I simply don't have any compulsion to cook them myself.

Pinto beans are another matter. I love them, cooked my way, and can make an entire meal from them, along with tomatoes and onions. Some people soak dried pinto beans overnight before cooking them, but that's not my way. I like to put them into water and cook them for a long time. Here's my method:

A.D.'s Pinto Beans

12-ounce package of pinto beans
hambone with some meat on it
water

The key to the quality of the beans is to have a hambone with some meat left on it. In fact, I seldom cook pinto beans unless I have a suitable hambone. The ham, of course, is cooked for its own sake, and I use the pinto bean dish as a means of finishing off the ham. Anyhow, put a hambone with some meat on it into a pot of suitable size. Cover with water. Wash the pinto beans and dump them into the pot. Bring to boil, then reduce heat, cover, and simmer for several hours. Check the water level from time to time. The pinto beans will absorb water and expand, and could easily burn on the bottom if the water level isn't maintained.

When the beans are tender, remove the cover and boil gently until the water cooks down and thickens. Watch the beans very closely during this stage.

Serve the beans onto plates directly from the pot. Also pull some meat off the bone and serve it with the beans. Eat with large sliced onions, chilled tomatoes, and cornbread or crackers. I also like pinto beans served with green onions, trimmed and kept in a glass or jar with ice water. If I don't have vine-ripened tomatoes, I'll take them canned. I put the can into the refrigerator long enough to chill it thoroughly. When I am ready to serve, I remove the top of the can, drink off the juice, and dump the tomatoes onto plates. I'll allow half a 16-ounce can per person.

The above recipe, I think, comes from the Campbells on my father's side of the family. I doubt that it came from my mother's people. The DuPrees, they don't fart.

Leftover pinto beans can be frozen and used later in a chili dish, or they can be made into refried beans and served as a side dish, or used in various Mexican creations, such as tacos. Here's what you'll need:

Refried Beans

leftover pinto beans
bacon drippings
clove of garlic

Crush a clove of garlic and sauté it. Heat bacon drippings in a large frying pan and sauté garlic for a few minutes. Add leftover beans and mash them while they are "frying." Cook for about 10 minutes.

You may also want to use leftover beans, or leftover refried leftover beans, in a dip.

Bean Dip

2 cups refried beans
1 cup sour cream
2 pickled jalapeño peppers
1 tablespoon Monterey jack cheese, grated

Mix refried beans and sour cream. Mince 2 pickled jalapeño peppers and mix in with beans and cream. Put into a serving bowl and sprinkle with grated Monterey jack cheese. Dip with tortilla chips.

Cowboy Beans

The cowboys had a good recipe for dried pinto beans that had been soaked overnight in water. Here's how it goes:

1 pound dried pinto beans
½ pound salt pork
1 medium onion, chopped
1 or 2 jalapeño peppers
1 small can tomato paste (6-ounce size)

Soak beans in water overnight. When you are ready to cook and have a good fire, drain the beans and put them into a Dutch oven. Cover with new water and add other ingredients. (The salt pork can be cut into chunks, or it can be used in a whole strip; when used whole, however, it is best to cut longways and shortways down to the rind, like a checkerboard.) Bring to boil, then cover and simmer for an hour.

If you've got some DuPrees or other prim folks coming for dinner, you might consider cooking some beans that are of slightly more delicate consequence. I've always been fond of Boston baked beans, but I don't cook the dish and have no recipe to offer. I am also especially fond of black beans cooked with the aid of a crockpot. Here's my recipe:

Crock of Black Beans

A little salt pork goes a long way. But I love the flavor of the stuff, especially when it is used as seasoning for black beans, and I tend to use too much of it. Those people on a low-salt diet might cut back on it considerably.

> *2 cups dried black beans*
>
> *¼ pound salt pork, finely diced*
>
> *4½ cups water*
>
> *1 cup chopped onion*
>
> *¼ cup catsup*
>
> *¼ cup molasses*
>
> *2 tablespoons brown sugar*
>
> *1 teaspoon salt*
>
> *1 teaspoon ground (dry) mustard*

Put all the ingredients into the crockpot and stir. Turn heat to low, cover the crockpot, and cook for 10 to 12 hours. I like these beans, on the side, with chili. Serves 8 to 10.

Variation: Substitute blackeyed peas for black beans if you must, but be warned that there is a noticeable increase in flatus. Call in the Campbells.

If you are lucky enough to have access to fresh blackeyes (or similar peas), picked off the vine when green, be sure to try them, if you haven't already. Along with the mature peas, pick a few pods that haven't yet filled out. Snap these and add them to the pot right along with the shelled peas. (Fresh frozen peas can also be used, but aren't quite as good as those fresh from the vine.) Merely shell the peas, wash them, and boil them in a pot with water and seasoning meat until tender. There are dozens of kinds of such peas, and all are good, at least to me.

You might also consider cooking an old favorite, using fresh peas:

Hoppin' John

2 cups blackeyed peas, fresh or fresh-frozen

1 ham hock (with quite a bit of meat)

1 medium onion, diced

1 stalk celery, chopped

water

salt and pepper to taste

1 cup rice

Put peas, ham hock, onion, celery, salt, and pepper into a suitable pot with 2½ cups of water. Bring to boil, cover, reduce heat, and simmer for an hour, or until the peas are tender. While the peas are simmering, cook 1 cup of rice in a separate pot with 2 cups of boiling water and a little salt. When water comes to boil again, reduce heat, cover, and cook for 20 minutes. After 20 minutes, take rice off the heat. When the peas are done, pull the meat from the ham hock, chop it, and mix it into the peas. Mix in the cooked rice. Simmer for a few minutes, then serve.

ONIONS

I never did realize how heavily we depend on onions until I started putting together all my recipes for *Outdoor Life's Complete Fish & Game Cookbook.* Just about every good stew or pot roast recipe calls for onions, and I hesitate to think of how many tons are used each year—and how many tears are shed while peeling, slicing, or chopping them.

I saw a cable TV show one day about Vidalia onions, named for a town in the state of Georgia. A spokesperson claimed that true Vidalia onions, when mature, are rather flat in shape and that they won't make you cry. Not long after that, I bought a bag of "genuine Vidalia" onions at a vegetable market while I was going to the Georgia side of West Point Lake to visit my brother, Ira L. Livingston, a retired Colonel.

The Colonel had a batch of onions under his house, which he had bought from somewhere in Texas. They looked like ordinary Bermuda onions to me, but he said they beat Vidalia onions every time. I also remember that my mother always talked about Vidalia onions, since she was from Unidilla, Georgia—but most of the onions we ate at home were raised from plants that she ordered from Onion, Texas.

Anyhow, I tested the Vidalia onions, and I'm happy to report that they are indeed good—and that they truly won't make you shed too many tears, if, that is, you've got the real thing. Also, I learned from another TV show that putting onions into the freezer shortly before using them will also reduce the tears. Damned if it doesn't.

The color of an onion isn't without importance. Usually, yellow onions are stronger than white. The red/purple onions are usually mild, and they make a happy edition to salads, not only because of the mild flavor but also because of the color. But be warned that red onions are not always mild. I've bought some in supermarkets that were quite strong.

For the most part, onions are used in a salad or in a dish of meat or other vegetables. But they can stand their own, and here's a few recipes.

Crockpot Onions

Don't let the simplicity of this dish fool you. It's good. It's foolproof. And what could be easier to prepare?

mild onions of medium size
salt and pepper
butter

Put the unpeeled onions into the crockpot. That's right. Unpeeled. Turn to low and cook for 10 to 12 hours. Remove the onions, peel while still hot, cut in half, salt and pepper to taste, and dab with a little butter. Serve as a vegetable, along with meat, bread, and other vegetables of your choice.

Note: Large onions can also be used for this recipe, but these don't fit nicely into the crockpot and might require longer cooking times.

Onion Rings

My son Bill won't even touch a raw onion, much less eat one, but the boy is fond of fried onion rings. He especially likes them along with hot dogs or chili dogs. I've never run a test, but think he would eat a number 2 washtub full of onion rings, along wih 7 or 8 hotdogs. Here's what you'll need for my recipe:

large mild onions
cooking oil
½ cup buttermilk
½ cup all purpose flour

I prefer to use the wide, flat onions simply because they make large rings. I peel them and slice them ¼-inch thick. Then I separate the outer rings, saving the inner wheel pieces to eat raw.

Heat about 2 inches of oil in a large frying pan. Dip the rings one at a time in buttermilk, then into flour. Carefully put the rings into the pan and fry on medium heat for several minutes, or until the rings are lightly browned. Drain well on absorbent paper. Don't try to cook too many at a time.

One of my favorite culinary treats doesn't fit too well in a recipe book because it's a little difficult to pin down. I'm talking about the wild onion. My first experience with these came about years ago, when I found some nice ones growing on the embankment leading from the road down to Spring Creek, a stream that helps feed Lake Seminole. I pulled up a few, peeled them, chopped them, and added them to scrambled eggs. Since then, I have started using wild onions and wild garlics in many, many dishes. One problem, however, is that some of these are very, very strong, and others are not. Experience is the only guide, and it is hoped that the simple recipe below will be inspirational.

Eggs & Onions

chicken eggs
wild onions with tops
salt and pepper
butter

Peel the onions and chop them, along with part of the green tops. Break the eggs into a bowl and beat very lightly, just to mix the whites and yolks. Melt a little butter in a cast iron frying pan. Sauté a few of the chopped onions for several minutes. Stir in the eggs. Heat until the eggs set, stirring constantly. Salt and pepper the eggs to taste. Serve with buttered toast, crisp bacon, and sliced vine-ripened tomatoes.

Note: If you don't have any wild onions at hand, ride up and down a country road for a few miles, looking for plants with onion-like leaves, which are usually hollow. If you find something that looks like an onion, has a bulb like an onion, and smells like an onion, or garlic, you've got onion or garlic. If you don't have time to hunt for wild foods, try the green onions that are available all the year in supermarkets.

Braised Onions

This dish is best when it is cooked with small onions, about an inch in diameter. But a larger size can be used, if necessary.

small onions
butter

sugar

salt

water

Peel the onions and put them into a little salted water. Do not cover. Bring to boil and cook until the onions are very tender. Most of the water should boil off. Reduce heat and add a little butter and sugar. Simmer and turn the onions until they are browned.

I got the recipe above from Marjorie Kinnan Rawlings's *Cross Creek Cookery*. Mrs. Rawlings said that it is marvelous with duck or goose, and she recommended that the brown juice be served with the onions. I also like the dish with a large hamburger steak.

I haven't said enough in this chapter about the onion— and almost nothing about the garlic, and first cousins such as the leek and the ramp. As stated earlier, however, the onion is important mainly because it adds flavor to other dishes. Almost all meat dishes, stews, and hashes benefit from onions. In some dishes, they become a true partner, as in the following recipe:

Liver and Onions

sliced onion

calf's liver

bacon

flour

salt

pepper

Fry the bacon in a skillet and set aside to drain. Pour off some of the bacon drippings. Slice the liver about½ inch thick and trim. Salt and pepper the liver slices, then roll them in flour. Sauté in bacon drippings until browned on both sides. This will take about 7 minutes on medium heat. Do not overcook. Pour the rest of the bacon drippings into the frying pan, bring to heat, and sauté the onion slices until they are tender. Serve a slice of onion on top of each slice of liver, topping with a strip of bacon.

CORN AND POTATOES

After I had a somewhat heated telephone conversation with a New York editor concerning the chicken eggs that I had specified in a recipe, she got started on Irish potatoes. She had never heard of *Irish* potatoes, she said.

"Well, Irish potatoes are not sweet potatoes," I said.

"Sweet potatoes?"

"Perhaps you, er, people call sweet potatoes yams. Sweet potatoes are not true yams, but they are similar to yams. Irish potatoes aren't yams, either. Nor are they new potatoes."

"New potatoes?"

"New potatoes are potatoes that are usually harvested before the plant is fully mature," I said. "The potatoes are kind of small and reddish."

"Red potatoes, then."

"Well, not necessarily. I don't think that all red potatoes are really new potatoes. I'm not sure. But we are getting off the point. The potatoes that I'm talking about in the recipe are like regular baking potatoes. Idaho potatoes, maybe."

"Then they are regular potatoes?" she said.

"Absolutely," I said.

"Then let's just call them potatoes," she said.

"That's fine," I said after a suitable silence. I was paying for the long distance phone call.

"I take it that you don't agree?" she said.

"I really don't care what you call Irish potatoes," I said, "Just as long as you do not specify sweet potatoes or Rock of Gibraltar potatoes."

"Of course not," she said, as if she knew everything there is to know about Rock of Gibraltar potatoes. I doubt that she had peeled more than 500 pounds of spuds during her entire life.

I'm no potato expert either, but, on the other hand, I *have* peeled some 67,000 pounds of potatoes, give or take a ton or so of Rock of Gibraltar potatoes, while serving up a hitch in the U.S. Navy. On our ship, the potatoes were kept in special bins topside, and, before peeling them, I had to first get them down two sets of ladders to the galley. This was usually done at night so that the ship's crew would have plenty of sliced potatoes ready for breakfast.

Actually, peeling the potatoes, then slicing them, dicing them, or making fingers for French frying wasn't hard, especially since I had machinery to use. We had a mechanical "peeler," for example, that ground away the surfaces pretty well if you left them in the machine long enough. If you took them out too quickly, the spuds still contained a good many eyes. I always had to work over mine with a paring knife, digging out the eyes, because I couldn't bear to grind half the potatoes away in the machine. There were too many hungry people in the world, I thought, to be grinding away the potato meat.

Luckily for the ship's crew, my personal conservation of potatoes and taxpayers' dollars saved the day. While we were headed for the Mediterranean Sea, taking the North Atlantic route, we met a supply ship, but, unfortunately, our potatoes had been misrouted or otherwise misplaced. This had the Commissary Officer mighty worried, and my guess is that he forgot to order spuds. Because I had conserved potatoes, however, he told the Captain, Steady Eddie, that we had plenty of spuds to last us until we reached the Rock of Gibraltar. Then the Commissary Officer told me that I had to peel the potatoes by hand just to make sure that our supply lasted until we reached the Rock.

I did it without a grumble, although I was often peeling potatoes all night long. Well, when we got to the Rock, our

potatoes were not waiting for us. Where they were, nobody

knows. However, there just happened to be a large store of local potatoes on the Rock. Unfortunately for me, the U.S. Navy bought them. These things were about the size of a golf ball and just as hard. The machine wouldn't peel them, and doing it by hand took too long. They were also dirty, and made a mess. And they were tough, making them difficult to slice, dice, or finger. But of course I struggled along with these small potatoes simply because I wanted everybody to have enough to eat.

Our original shipment of potatoes, together with a new shipment, had been sent on to Naples and were waiting for us at that port. Now, suddenly, in a military manner, we had more potatoes than we needed. These stateside potatoes, probably from Idaho, were about the prettiest things I had ever seen. They were six or seven inches long. Clean, tender, and juicy. But the U.S. Navy said I couldn't use them until all the Gibraltar spuds were gone. The Commissary Officer knew what I had been up against, and knew about my heroic efforts to ward off hunger aboard ship. He told me how sorry he was. Nonetheless he said that I had to use up the Gibraltar spuds first. I told him that if we didn't eat some of those stateside potatoes, they would ruin before we got to them, especially since we had more than we could store properly. He knew that, but, nonetheless, we had to follow U.S. Navy potato regulations.

Well, that was that, it seemed. At the next mail call, however, I happened to see a front page newspaper article about farmers burning potatoes in the American midwest. Tons and tons of perfectly good potatoes were going up in smoke—and not a Gibraltar spud among them. That did it. On a dark night, a squawl made up and I figured it would keep Steady Eddie and the rest of the officers off the topside decks. I eased my way up the ladder and unlocked the potato bin that held the last of the Gibraltar spuds. Although the ship was rolling from side to side, I shouldered a 100-pound bag and got my footing with it. Then, when the ship rolled to port, I went with the roll and dumped the sack of potatoes overboard. Anyone who doesn't believe that this was tricky business should shoulder a hundred pound bag and walk across a ship's deck, topside, at night, during a storm. But I made it, timing my release just right, freeing my hands just in time to stay myself at the railing.

"Plop" went the bag when it hit the Mediterranean. I didn't think anybody could hear it, but nevertheless I held my breath for a long while. Nobody toward the stern yelled "man overboard," and I proceeded, on wobbly legs, with another 100-pound bag. And another. Finally, the bin was empty—and I hadn't been caught. The next day, my legs were so sore that I could barely walk, but the ship's company enjoyed prime stateside potatoes and I finished in time to get a little sleep.

So, after having peeled some 67,000 pounds of stateside potatoes, not to mention the Rock of Gibraltar spuds, I can say for certain that it saves a lot of time (and potato meat) to leave the skin on when making French fries, diced potatoes, or sliced potatoes. The peeling, after all, contains lots of vitamins and other such things that are good for you. So, I recommend that you leave the skin on potatoes, except possibly for making mashed potatoes.

On the other hand, I recently saw a piece on TV that warned against eating potato skins. I didn't want to hear it, and shut the TV off. The trouble here is not only that the "experts" give out conflicting advice, but also that various warnings are blown way out of proportion. For example, I read in a book that sassafras tea contained some substance that might be dangerous to your health, and that the F.D.A. had banned the use of sassafras root in herbal teas. Reluctantly, I quit drinking my usual cup or two of sassafras tea each spring. Then I read, in another book, that it would take 1,200 pounds of sassafras per day to hurt you! So, pass the sassafras and eat the potato skins. Which brings us to my first recipe:

A.D.'s Potato Skins

Most people won't eat all of a baked potato. They scoop out a little, and leave the rest to be thrown away. Don't do it. Save them for the next day. Or, cook this dish and save the scooped out part for mashed potatoes.

stateside baking potatoes
melted butter
salt and pepper
grated cheese

Heat the oven to 350 degrees. Bake the potatoes in the center of the oven for an hour, or until they are soft and ready to eat. Cool. Cut the potatoes in half lengthwise. Scoop out part of the pulp and save it for mashed potatoes or some other dish. (As indicated above, leftover baked potatoes can also be used.) I like to have about a quarter of an inch of potato left on the skin.

Preheat the broiler. Brush the potato skins, inside and out, lightly with butter. Salt and pepper to taste. Cut the skin a little on each end and flatten. Arrange the halves on a suitable rack, meat side up. Sprinkle lightly with grated cheese. Broil until the cheese browns nicely. Eat while hot.

When I was in college, a short order cook who worked the late night shift at some joint on University Row served up lots of hash brown potatoes. They were quite good, but I think we bought them just to see the guy toss a panful into the air and catch every one. He used, I might add, diced potatoes instead of patties made with grated potatoes and egg. I confess that I cook mine in a wok type fry pan (which has a cover) and stir them from time to time. In any case, the recipe below borrows from a dish that L.L. Bean was

144

fond of cooking according to *The L.L. Bean Game & Fish Cookbook*. Here's my version, which I make with diced potatoes cooked in a wok type stir-fry pan.

Hash Browns

5 or 6 cups diced potatoes
2 cups diced onions
1 tablespoon diced parsley
½ pound finely diced salt pork
salt and pepper

Cut the salt pork into bacon-like slices and remove the rind. Cut each slice into three strips, longways, then dice them. In a large frying pan or wok, sauté the diced pork until crisp, then drain it and set aside. Sauté the onions for 5 minutes. Add the potatoes, parsley, salt, and pepper. Cover tightly and simmer the potatoes on low heat for 20 minutes. Remove the cover, add the salt pork, and turn heat to high. Brown the potatoes as best you can, turning or not turning, depending on your skill as a chef or hash brown man. Serves 4.

Variation: One of my favorite fish dishes also involves salt pork and potatoes. I got it from the fish cookery that has developed in the Outer Banks region of North Carolina, and it called for potatoes and fish that had been boiled separately and mixed on serving plates. (This recipe is covered in my book *Outdoor Life's Complete Fish & Game Cookbook*.) The same flavor can be caught by dicing a fish fillet or two. Brown the diced fish after the cooked salt pork has been set aside. Then drain the fish and set aside until the potatoes have been cooked. Mix fish and diced salt pork back into the potatoes.

I talked once with a magazine editor who said he liked to visit his grandfather so that he could eat those little round potatoes. He was talking about new potatoes, which are usually boiled with suitable meat seasoning. They are indeed good. Usually, folks who have their own gardens can dig (with a large spoon) a few new potatoes from around the potato stalk or root systems without killing the plant. Thus, new potatoes can be enjoyed before the main harvest. At times, they can be purchased at the market. Any small potato, ranging in size from a golf ball to a tennis ball, will do for the following recipe.

Tangy New Potatoes

Here's a recipe that I borrowed from Lea & Perrins, a firm that markets Worcestershire sauce—including a new white wine Worcestershire sauce.

1 pound new potatoes
½ cup white wine Worcestershire sauce
¼ cup melted butter
salt and pepper to taste
paprika

Wash the new potatoes and cut into ¼-inch slices. No need to peel. Turn on the oven broiler. Melt butter in a sauce pan. Dip potato slices in melted butter, sprinkle both sides with salt, pepper, and paprika. Arrange the potato slices on a broiling rack and place 3 inches from the heat source. Broil for 3 minutes, turn and broil for 3 minutes on the other side, or until the potatoes are golden brown.

Fried Sweet Potatoes

This sweet potato dish is very easy to prepare. One of my aunts cooked it for me when I visited her, possibly because she liked it herself but was afraid to reach into the "hill" for potatoes. Back then, we stored potatoes in the ground. First a pit was dug. This was lined with straw. Then the potatoes were piled on top of the straw floor. Another layer of straw was added, then another layer of potatoes. The bin was covered at ground level with sheets of tin, which in turn were covered with dirt. A slanted hole was dug into the hill, and thus one had to reach into the hole and feel around for potatoes. Trouble was, rattlesnakes also liked to den up in potato hills—or I thought they did. Before reaching into the hill, I always stuck a tree branch into the hole and swished it around considerably, pausing from time to time, to listen for a telltale rattle.

sweet potatoes

butter

brown sugar

Peel the sweet potatoes and slice them, lengthwise, about ¼-inch thick. Heat a little butter in a frying pan, or on a griddle, and sauté the potato slices until browned on the down side. Turn the slice over and brown the other side. When the potato slices are browned on both sides, and seem to be tender when tested with a fork, sprinkle lightly with brown sugar and cook for another minute or two.

Note: Leftover baked sweet potatoes can also be cooked, to great advantage, by the above procedure. The slices will have to be thicker, and the cooking time won't be as long.

Baked Sweet Potatoes

Baked sweet potatoes are hard to beat, and they can be kept without refrigeration for several days. My mother often baked a large batch, then left them in the oven until she wanted one. She would warm these up to eat at meals, and sometimes the children would snitch one and eat it cold.

medium-sized sweet potatoes
bacon drippings
butter

Preheat the oven to 450 degrees. Wash the sweet potatoes and dry them with a cloth. Rub each potato well with bacon drippings. Put potatoes on a rack in the center of the oven and cook for 50 minutes. Large sweet potatoes may require a little more time. When they are done, the reddish meat of the potato will shrink, leaving a rather loose skin that is very easy to peel. For serving, peel the potatoes and put a slit in them lengthwise. Put some butter in the slit. I prefer fresh butter with baked sweet potatoes, although margarine will certainly do.

Camp Variation: Sweet potatoes can be covered with hot coals raked out from a campfire and cooked until tender, or they can be buried in the ground before the campfire is built. They don't have to be wrapped with aluminum foil.

A lot of people like fresh corn cooked in the shucks, and I've eaten some good shuck-covered corn that had been roasted over coals or in campfire ashes. For atmosphere, of course, a live fire and hot coals and genuine shucks are highly desireable, but for flavor I would not count out corn that has been properly cooked in a crockpot. I cook it in two ways:

Crockpot Corn

5 or 6 ears of fresh corn, not too ripe
butter
salt or garlic salt
pepper

Shuck the corn and clean the ears. If necessary, cut off the small ends so that the ears will fit into your crockpot. Melt the butter. Tear off some sheets of aluminum foil. Coat each ear with melted butter, sprinkle it with salt and pepper, then seal it in foil. Use the so-called drugstore fold instead of merely wrapping the aluminum foil around the corn and twisting the ends. Stand the ears up in the crockpot. Cover, turn the heat to low, and cook for 10 hours or longer. An hour or so before eating, reverse the ears so that the butter will be more evenly distributed.

Easy Crockpot Corn

6 or 7 ears of corn
butter
salt

Remove the silks from the end of the corn but leave the shucks on. Cut off both ends so that the ears will fit in the pot. Fit 6 or 7 ears around the pot and cover. Turn to high heat for 1 hour, then cook on low for 2 hours.

Take the corn out of the pot, shuck it, and remove the inside strands of silk. Have butter and salt at hand for those who want it.

Boiled Corn on the Cob

fresh corn
butter
sugar
water

Shuck the corn, pull out the silks, and trim the ends. Bring a *large* pot of water to boil and add a little sugar—just enough to contribute to the term "sweet corn." Add the corn and boil for 10 or 12 minutes. Drain and put a whole ear, hot, onto each plate. Serve with plenty of soft butter. If you don't have real butter at hand, try mayonnaise. It's easy to spread—and tastes good, too.

Aunt Shelley's Creamed Corn

My Aunt Shelley was fond of telling a story about her 2-year-old granddaughter saying, at Sunday dinner, "Pass the corn." Just like a grown person, Aunt Shelley always added. I won't show old family photographs here, but the corn was indeed worth passing for another helping or two. The secret, I think, for this and similar recipes is having very fresh corn, picked from the stalk at the right time, and cut from the cob as follows: Shuck the ears and pull out the silks; then, with a very sharp knife and a sure hand, slice off the tops of the kernels. Slice around the ear again, cutting a little more off the kernels. Then scrape the cobs with the back of the knife. This method will produce lots of pulp and juice, which is mixed right in with the kernel pieces. Here's what you'll need:

12 ears fresh corn, young and tender
½ cup bacon drippings
¼ cup sugar
1 tablespoon butter
1 teaspoon salt
4 cups of water

Cut and scrape the corn from the ears as described above. Heat the bacon drippings in a frying pan and sauté the corn for 5 or 6 minutes. In a suitable pot, preferably ceramic or porcelain-lined, bring to boil 4 cups of water. Add corn, sugar, butter, and salt. Cook on low heat for 30 to 40 minutes, stirring almost constantly. *Warning*: this dish will burn or scorch on the bottom if it isn't watched carefully and stirred frequently.

Corn Fritters

To prepare this dish, cut the corn from the cob as described above—but do not scrape off the pulp and juice.

1 cup corn off cob
bacon drippings
1 egg
¼ cup flour
salt and pepper

Beat the egg in a bowl and mix in corn, flour, salt, and pepper. The mixture should drop out of a spoon like pancake batter. On a flat grill or pancake griddle, fry a couple of strips of bacon. Drain bacon and save. Using a large spoon, drop corn fritters onto the griddle. Fry the fritters for a few minutes in the bacon drippings on medium heat, then flip them over and cook the other side. Both sides should be nicely browned.

Bill's Choice

When my son Bill was just a tot, he said he wanted his corn off the cob. I suppose that he had teething problems, or just didn't have time to fool with gnawing an ear all the way. What the boy wanted, of course, was whole kernel corn, cooked without diced bell peppers, lima beans, and other things that had to be fished out. Anyhow, this is what resulted from his request:

whole kernel corn

olive oil

garlic

salt

I normally use either frozen corn or canned corn for this dish, but fresh corn can also be used provided that you get most of the kernel on the first cut and don't scrape the cob. (Try using a small knife and cut between the rows of kernels, angling the blade a bit. Then cut the other side.) If you've got frozen corn, thaw it out and drain it well. If you've got canned whole kernel corn, drain it, rinse off the corn in cool water, and drain well. Peel a couple of cloves of garlic and cut in half. Heat a little olive oil in a wok or frying pan and sauté the garlic for a few minutes without Bill seeing it. Discard the garlic. Increase the heat to high, add the corn, and stir-fry for several minutes. Salt to taste.

Variation: In spite of what Bill thinks about it, this dish will gain considerably in color if you will dice up a red bell pepper along with the corn.

Popcorn

American movies and popcorn have gone together for a good many years. At one time, a man could take his family out to the movies at a reasonable price. But, unfortunately, this is no longer the case. The American father with ordinary income simply can't afford to take his wife and three or four kids to the movies. I'm talking not only about the price of admission to the movie house but also about the price of the popcorn and other refreshments. It's outrageous. I realize that there is an economic side to all this, but I don't understand it and don't want to. All I know for sure is that the American way has changed.

For better or worse, TV and cable TV have brought the movie to our living rooms, dens, and bedrooms. But we need not suffer from the lack of popcorn. The next time you are at the supermarket, pick up a couple of packages. You can pop a tubful for practically nothing. You don't have to use special poppers either. An ordinary pot or Dutch oven will do, and we sometimes make a quick batch in a wok or half-wok. It's a wok-shaped frying pan, with a handle and lid. Since the bottom part is narrow, it works nicely for holding and heating the oil and unpopped kernels. Just shake it from time to time until all the popping stops. Take it off the heat, remove the lid, and sprinkle on a little salt. Add butter only if you have no fat or cholesterol problems, and have the will power to keep your hand out of the popcorn bowl when the plot thickens.

AN OLD SEMINOLE SECRET REVEALED

Why some people call mudfish "cypress trout" has always been a mystery to me. I don't have any trouble with the *cypress* part of the name, since a cypress swamp is one of the mudfish's favorite hangouts. But *trout?* Any self-respecting mudfish would laugh at a dainty size 14 Royal Coachman or Light Cahill, and wouldn't even bother to rise during a hatch of gnats. These mudfish want meat, and they are especially fond of lures tipped with pork rind. They will eat a Snagless Sally just to get at a #2 pork frog, then spit out hook, wire, and spinner blade, all bent up beyond further use. Cypress trout? Nobody is going to get a 10-pound mudfish out of cypress roots with a flyrod. Not even Stu Apte can do that.

Experts call them bowfin, scientists call them *Amia calva*, but most anglers know them as blackfish, grinnel, dogfish, or, more commonly, mudfish. They aren't mud cats, however, and should not be confused with catfish or bullheads. That would be like comparing a kitten to a bobcat, a night crawler to a rattlesnake. These mudfish are tough and don't quit. They'll twist right out the bottom of a landing net. In their range, which is extensive, they have no doubt torn up more tackle than any other species of comparable-size fish. Millions upon millions of lures, set hooks, and limb lines have been twisted, straightened, broken, or otherwise torn up by mudfish. They terrorize bass anglers in some regions, such as the lower part of the Apalachicola River, and many of the bass tournament boys carry clubs to conk them with.

154

I know one big fellow, mean enough to be a linebacker for the Chicago Bears, who is literally afraid of mudfish. He packs a snub-nosed .38 pistol in his tackle box to deal with them.

Looking for trouble, the fish ranges up and down the Mississippi drainage system, slowed down on the West by the Rocky Mountains. They could no doubt go on into California, if they wanted to. Or they could go up through North Dakota and cross the border into Canada, if they wanted to. The mudfish is, for the most part, however, a Southerner.

My brother, Jim Livingston, spent a good part of his life hating the mudfish. Always a lover of swamp or bottomland angling, his main purpose was to put meat on the table. To him, that's what fishing was all about. But the mudfish stumped him and often confounded him. To be sure, a number of people eat the things, after first bleeding the meat or treating it in one manner or another. Jim tried everything, including a marinade of sulfuric acid, but the meat always resembled cotton in texture and tasted none too good. Finally, while living in a small house beside a big lake in Florida, Jim came up with *the* definitive recipe for fried mudfish. If I remember correctly, he based his recipe on ancient tribal secrets that he finagled from a down-and-out Seminole Indian at a bingo game somewhere south of Lake Okeechobee. Historical notes aside, here's all you need to fry juicy, palpable mudfish every time:

1 whole mudfish, about 5 pounds (no larger)
peanut oil
white corn meal, water-ground style
salt and pepper
1 young tomato plant about 8 inches high

As soon as you get the mudfish out of the water, don't waste time trying to bleed the thing. Don't try to skin it or scale it or gut it, either. As soon as possible, dig a hole at least 3 feet deep beside a young tomato plant that is exposed to the morning sun. Insert the mudfish into the hole. Cover it well with dirt, and pack the mound tightly so that the mudfish can't get out. Use posthole diggers if you've got them, being careful not to wallow out the sides more than necessary. Remember that even a 15-pound mudfish will fit neatly into a normal post hole of suitable depth. *Always* insert the mudfish into the hole head first, so that any wiggling would tend to make it go deeper instead of out. If the fish is put into damp ground, it's best to cover the hole with plenty of rocks or brickbats for at least a week.

Let the mudfish hole simmer in the morning sun until the tomato plant puts on fruit. Pull off 3 green tomatoes when they are mature in size (2 to 3 inches in diameter) but haven't started turning red. Slice these green tomatoes into rings about ½-inch thick. Heat an inch or so of peanut oil in a large frying pan. Whisk the egg in a small bowl, adding just a tad of water. Stir the salt and pepper into the flour, then spread the mixture onto a plate. Dip each tomato slice in the beaten egg, then flip-flop it in the corn meal mixture. Fry the tomato slices over medium heat until brown, turning once. Drain on absorbent paper. Eat while hot. Serves 4 or 5.

Note: Some old timey Florida crackers insist that all fried fish be eaten with grits, but some other Southerners in perfectly good standing might choose French fries. Also, many otherwise good people in various parts of the country prefer to fry fish in yellow corn meal, and some even prefer flour. Either of these ingredients will work pretty well in the above recipe, if substitution is necessary.

Warning: The recipe above depends upon starting with a well-rooted, healthy tomato plant at least 8 inches high. When using smaller plants, it might be wise to bleed the mudfish before burying it. This is accomplished by cutting the skin near the tail on both sides and leaving it in running water on a heavy-duty fish stringer for an hour or so. Also, remember that the measures above are for cooking a 5-pound mudfish. As with many other species, the smaller fish have a better flavor. Larger specimens are edible, to be sure, but they should be spaced equidistant between two tomato plants. Otherwise, the flavor might be a tad strong for modern tastes, although the Seminoles of old might well have doted on such fare.

Stirfried Green Tomatoes and Potatoes

Wok owners and stirfry freaks might well flip over this simple recipe. I can make a whole meal out of it.

green tomatoes

potatoes

onion

salt pork

black pepper

Dice the salt pork finely and brown it in a wok. Remove the pieces and set aside to drain. Dice the green tomatoes and potatoes. Chop the onion. Put tomatoes, potatoes, and onion into the wok and sprinkle lightly with pepper. Stir fry the vegetables in the pork fat until they are tender. Remove the vegetables from the wok and put them into a serving platter. Sprinkle with the salt pork pieces. Enjoy.

Broiled Tomatoes

I've always been fond of the flavor of cheese, tomatoes, and bacon, and the recipe below grew from a cheese toast topped with bacon and tomato.

large ripe tomatoes
Cheddar cheese, shredded
bacon

Slice the tomatoes. (Discard the end pieces, or save for another purpose.) Preheat the oven broiler. Fry the bacon in a frying pan until it is done but not quite crisp; break each slice of bacon in half and set aside. Arrange tomato slices on a wide broiling pan or cookie sheet. Broil 4 inches from heat source for a few minutes. Turn all the tomato slices over, sprinkle each slice with cheddar and top it with two of the halved bacon pieces. Broil until the cheese is melted and the bacon is crisp.

Variation: Spread mayonnaise on bread and use the broiled tomato slices, cheese, and bacon as filling for a sandwich.

Tomato, Ham, and Cheese Toast

Preheat the oven's broiler unit. Put a thin slice of boiled ham onto a slice of bread. Spread a little prepared mustard on the ham. Place a few thin strips of cheese on the ham, making a crisscross pattern. Put a thin slice of tomato atop the cheese. Broil close to heat source until the cheese melts.

BLT Sandwiches

I once knew an old farmer who tended the land owned by a rather wealthy Ford dealer. When the farmers in this part of the country made the big switch from mules to tractors, the sharecropper was pulled into the act and became something of a right-hand man for the dealer, who, it was said, sold more Ford tractors than any other dealer in the world. The two traveled widely on business and pleasure. But the farmer never got the hang of business, and, one felt, he had rather stay at home than travel. One day, while talking about food, he said, "I have et in New Orleans, Tampa, New York City, and San Fran-cisco. But I'll tell you right now, if you're hungry it's hard to beat syrup and sausage and biscuits!"

I feel the same way about bacon, lettuce, and tomato sandwiches. I prefer to use plenty of mayonnaise and soft white bread, topped with slices of tomatoes, crisp lettuce, and bacon. Salt and pepper to taste. The real secret, of course, is to have tomatoes that have ripened on the vine. I sometimes eat too many of these BLTs in summer, when big red tomatoes are plentiful. In recent years, I have switched to a low calorie and zero cholesterol mayonnaise. But I still spread it generously onto my bread.

VEGETABLE SOUPS AND GREEN SALADS

Many thrifty family cooks make soup with leftover vegetables. I endorse the practice, but, if I be honest, I'll have to say that the best soups, it seems to me, are made with fresh or fresh-frozen vegetables. Leftovers or canned vegetables, after simmering in a soup, tend to be too soft, and the soup is mushy. But maybe some soups are supposed to be that way, and, further, I realize that there's a thin line between soups and stews.

Thin lines aside, one of the best and more hearty of such dishes contains barley along with meat and vegetables. Health food freaks ought to eat more barley, a whole grain with nothing added or taken away from it. One of my favorite soups calls for beef along with barley and vegetables.

Barley, Beef, and Vegetable Soup

1½ pounds lean beef, diced

1 tablespoon peanut oil

1 medium onion, chopped

1 clove garlic, minced

1 can tomatoes (16-ounce size)

1 package frozen soup vegetables (16-ounce size)

> *½ cup pearled barley*
> *5 beef bouillon cubes*
> *5 cups hot water*
> *½ teaspoon basil leaves*
> *1 teaspoon salt*
> *½ teaspoon pepper*

Heat the oil in a stovetop Dutch oven and sauté the onions and garlic for 4 or 5 minutes. Add the beef and stir until browned. Dissolve the bouillon cubes in hot water and add to the Dutch oven. Turn the heat to high. Add the barley and the juice from the can of tomatoes. Then mash or chop the tomatoes and add them to the Dutch oven along with frozen vegetables, basil leaves, salt, and pepper. Bring to boil, reduce heat, cover, and simmer for an hour. Stir from time to time, and add a little water if needed. Serve this hearty soup with lots of good hot bread. I like the small loaves of French bread, with an individual loaf, buttered, for each plate.

In the above recipe, I usually dice the meat into ½-inch squares. If you want a stew instead of a soup, cut the beef into larger chunks.

You don't have to be a surgeon to bone out a venison shoulder or a leg of lamb cleanly. But you do need a sharp knife and a good eye. I had neither when I first concocted my recipe for venison bone and vegetable soup. In fact, a dull knife and the fact that my glasses had been misplaced somewhere no doubt contributed to the success of the dish. In short, I left some meat on the bones.

> *venison bones, with some meat*
> *1 large onion, diced*

1 stalk celery, diced

1 large potato, diced

1 large turnip, diced

1 large carrot, diced

4 large tomatoes, diced (or a 16-ounce can)

1 tablespoon parsley, chopped

2 teaspoons salt

1 teaspoon pepper

water

Saw the bones in half (or crack them) and fit them into a large iron pot or stove-top Dutch oven. Cover the bones with water, bring to a boil, reduce heat, cover, and simmer for two hours. Remove the bones, cool, and pull off the meat with a fork. Leave 3 cups of stock in the pot, and put the meat in with it. (Add enough water to make up 3 cups if necessary.) Add all other ingredients. Cover. Cook on low heat for an hour or so. Keep an eye on the liquid level, and add a little hot water if you want a thinner soup. Serve hot with crackers or bread of your choice.

Variation: Use other fresh or fresh-frozen vegetables of your choice. Try whole kernel corn or okra. If you've got surplus vine-ripened tomatoes, use 9 or 10 of them and add a little thyme.

Easy Variation: Use a 16-ounce package of frozen vegetable soup mix, 1 can of tomatoes (16-ounce size), and 1 tablespoon parsley. Salt and pepper to taste.

Camp Variation: Boning a deer or other large game in camp will reduce the bulk and the weight of the meat that you have to transport. Or, if weight is no great consideration, you may want to bone a shoulder just to prepare this recipe. Put the bones into a Dutch oven or other suitable pot and cover them with branch water. Add 1 package (6.1-ounce size) of dried vegetable Soup Starter. (This Soup Starter, packaged by Borden, Inc., is available in most grocery stores. It is compact, easy to carry, and requires no refrigeration.) Bring the water to boil. Cover and simmer until the meat comes off the bones easily. (Check the pot from time to time to see whether more water is needed.) Chop the meat and put it back into the pot. Add salt and pepper to taste. Simmer until the vegetables are ready. The total simmering time is about an hour and a half. It's worth the wait!

A local character of my acquaintance, somewhat tongue-tied, once traveled into another state with relatives. After driving a distance of some 60 miles overland, they stopped the car at a wayside cafe for breakfast. He couldn't read the menu, so he merely ordered ham and eggs. The waitress asked him how he liked his eggs. "I like 'em a lot," he said.

I feel pretty much the same way about salads, any way they are made. I like 'em a lot even when lettuce and tomatoes and such are merely tossed together. My only requirement, apart from a reasonble mix, is that everything be fresh and crisp. Although crisp lettuce is really all you need for a salad, most people add other greens and vegetables. I am especially fond of vine-ripened tomatoes, sliced and diced, in a tossed salad. I am also fond of using a little raw cauliflower, which adds a nice crunch as well as flavor.

In my opinion, dressings and bread or a few crackers on the side are essential for a really good salad. I like a simple oil and vinegar dressing, along with thin wheat crackers with seeds on top. A boiled chicken egg or two with plenty of salad makes a nice lunch, especially if the salad is topped with crumbled bacon or grated cheese.

Since I seldom toss a salad the same way twice, I don't have a recipe to set forth. Some rather fussy people say that

you've got to pull the lettuce apart with your hands in order to make good salad. But I usually end up chopping mine with a knife. I believe that the real secret is in having crisp lettuce, and to this end I would recommend that salad lovers buy a Tupperware lettuce crisper and use it always.

I'll admit that celery is not one of my favorite salad ingredients, and, when it is used, I want it well scraped to get rid of the strings. Also, I prefer the tender inner parts of the stalk for raw salads. I save the tough outer sticks and the green tops for cooking duck gumbo.

My favorite salad is Greek, which I started eating some years ago in small restaurants around Tarpon Springs, Florida, where my sister Phyllis lived. At that time, the sponge dock area had some tiny ethnic shops that sold feta cheese and olives out of the barrel. We would often purchase these and other ingredients, along with a loaf of Greek bread, and toss up a salad at Phyllis's house. The salad made a complete meal. Here's what we used:

Phyl's Greek Salad

lettuce

green onion

fresh tomatoes

anchovy fillets (canned)

black olives

feta cheese

olive oil and vinegar (for dressing)

salt and pepper to taste

Prepare the lettuce, green onions, and tomatoes as for a tossed green salad. Toss in a large bowl, then dress with | *164* oil, vinegar, salt, and freshly ground pepper. Put this tossed salad into large individual serving bowls. Top each serving with black olives, crumbled feta cheese, and two or more slices of anchovy fillets.

Note: My wife is also very fond of feta cheese. For safekeeping, she puts it into a widemouth jar, covers it with cold water, and puts it into my refrigerator. It'll keep for months—unless, in the heat of getting off on an early morning fishing trip, one doesn't mistake it for the jar of white pork rind and leave it in one's tacklebox for a few days in the back of one's pick-up truck. Feta, I have learned, has environmental limits.

Rachel's Choice

My sister Rachel had the advantage and used it well. In her yard grew a grapefruit tree and an avocado tree. She put them together.

1 grapefruit, ripe
1 avocado, ripe
mayonnaise (preferably home-made)
sweet Hungarian paprika (optional)

Cut the avocado in half and spoon out the meat in bite-size chunks. Peel the grapefruit and section it. Then peel each section and break the fruit into bite-sized pieces. (Taking the trouble to peel the sections, thereby getting the right texture, is the sort of detail that is necessary to make simple dishes great ones.) Mix the avocado chunks and grapefruit sections in a bowl of suitable size and top with good mayonnaise. Sprinkle on a little paprika for color.

I hate to end this chapter on a negative note, but now that President Bush has blown the whistle on broccoli, I feel that I must, on behalf of the school children of this great nation, tell the truth about cole slaw. This stuff, as served up in school lunchrooms for half a century, has turned too many young boys and girls against school as well as against vegetables and salads.

Back when I was in the fifth grade, an indelicate teacher by the name of Miss Gussie Willis made me eat a pile of this stuff from an aluminum tray. At that time, in our school, we had a kitchen but no mess hall. The students got their food at a line, then marched the tray back to their home room to eat it. Needless to say, spills and dropped trays were something of a problem, and one can understand why Miss Willis had a rule about cleaning up your tray. Clean trays, she said, didn't make messes in the room and hallways.

Well, I taught Miss Willis a thing or two about messes. One day, when I felt a little queasy even before lunch, she pushed her authority too far and forced me to mouth and swallow my cole slaw, which was especially watery on that particular day. I told the woman that I was sorry but, please, I somehow didn't feel well. I would feel better, she said, after I ate my good cole slaw. (She pronounced it "cold slaw," and I did, too.) I asked to be excused. She said I could go play after I finished my good cole slaw.

We had an hour for lunch, and the boys were in the habit of shooting marbles out under some pecan trees when we finished eating. Of course, everybody ate as quickly as possible. But I couldn't gulp down that cole slaw. Not that day. I sat there. I tried not to look at the cole slaw. But the smell was there. Outside the birds sang. I took a spoonful of the stuff and swallowed it. Outside the children played. Mouthful by mouthful the cole slaw went down. The last spoonful was almost all cabbage juice and soured mayonnaise, but I tried to swallow it anyway. My mouth filled with warm saliva. Up it came. All of it and more.

After almost half a century, the technique for making large-batch cole slaw has not changed. I still hate it, and, in fact, I can still smell the stuff. If it is too watery, which is the case more often than not, cole slaw is not only unfit for human consumption but will also contaminate perfectly good food on the same plate, platter, or tray. I've had more than one barbecue plate served with bread that was downright soggy with cole slaw juice.

I doubt that many readers—especially after reading the comments above—will make cole slaw very often for home consumption, but it is frequently made in large batches for serving up at family reunions, church suppers, fish fries, PTA fund raisers, and so on. Anyone making such a batch of cole slaw should first chop or shred the cabbage and put it into a good colander. Keep it in the colander for several hours, so that the cabbage juice will drain away and not accumulate in the bottom. Then, mix in a little mayonnaise just before serving. Never store this stuff in large containers, especially aluminum. Just in case, always serve cole slaw in a separate container, so that any juice that might seep out of it can't possibly get to the rest of the food.

Don't misunderstand me. I have nothing against cabbage, and I really love it steamed. Stuffed cabbage leaves can be great. Corned beef and cabbage, or, better, a New England boiled dinner, is really fine eating. When well drained, even sauerkraut is all right.

PART 3

A Drink or Two

ARDENT SPIRITS

Before I met James Travis, all I knew about the Irish was that they built sturdy American railroads, brewed rank whiskey, and wrote beautiful poetry. But now I know beyond a shadow of a doubt that Shakespeare was an Irishman, that Irish peddlers established the first trade route to China, and that, through their influence on Pythagoras, the Druids of Eire (not to be confused with the corrupt Druids of Gaul) blazed the way for Western mathematics.

Besides being the consummate Irishman, standing head and shoulders above the mere Boston barstool professional, Travis, an editor at a university press, has a sharp eye and a neat proofreader's curlicue. Amazingly and somewhat disconcertingly, he can start editing a piece of writing at the top of the page and immediately reach down to correct the spelling of a wayward word at the bottom. He has a Gestaltic eye, and any word out of proper configuration immediately pops out at him like neon.

I worked under Travis for a time and a very good time it was. One day, with an audience, I smiled when I told him that Irish whiskey is as raw as Arkansas moonshine. Sour mash bourbon, I claimed, is the stuff to sip on. Bourbon has a corn base, whereas Irish whiskey, as well as Scotch, is made mostly of barley. Scotch is brewed from all malted barley (sprouted barley) whereas the Irish is made from half malted and half unsprouted barley. Canadian whiskey is a blend of corn, rye, and barley brews. Anyhow, I argued before Travis that sour mash bourbon is by far the best whiskey, an esprit of the American way, for the same reason that sour dough makes the best of breads. Having made my spiel, I held up a cupped fist and made a toast to the Reverend Elijah Craig, Baptist, father of the modern bourbon distillery.

Well, the thing had gone a little too far for Travis, but, pulling a smirk, he held in his rage and spoke quietly. All *true* whiskey, he said, is Irish, and it is Saint Patrick, not the Reverend Elijah Craig, who should receive libation. Further, he claimed, the American word "whiskey" as well as the Scottish word "whisky" is from the Gaelic *uisge-beatha*, meaning "water of life." Thus spake Travis.

In any case, I'll have to allow that Irish coffee, if properly made, is surely one of the great pleasures of the Western world. Here's how I make mine:

Irish Coffee

hot, black coffee, 5½ ounces per serving
1½ ounces Irish whiskey per serving
1 teaspoon sugar per serving
heavy whipping cream
confectioner's sugar (for whipped cream)
vanilla extract (for whipped cream)

Whip some cream. Before starting, however, it's best to chill your bowl and your whisks or other beaters, as well as the cream itself. In warm weather, put the bowl on ice when you beat the cream. Pour a cup of heavy whipping cream into the bowl and start whisking it. As you go, slowly fold in 2 tablespoons of confectioner's sugar and ½ teaspoon of vanilla extract. Beat until the cream holds a soft peak and slides off a tablespoon in a nice glob. Don't make it too thick. (Never use a food processor or a blender to whip cream. An electic mixer can be used, but proceed cautiously unless you want homemade butter in your whipped cream. Start on a medium speed, then reduce it to low.) Put the whipped cream into the refrigerator until you are ready to proceed.

Brew some coffee. It ought to be fresh, hot, and strong. (For maximum pleasure, grind some coffee beans in a kitchen mill, filling the air with the aroma.) Coffee made in some electric percolators isn't hot enough, and most people make such coffee far too weak. Weak coffee won't do in Irish whiskey. After you have brewed strong coffee, pour some hot water into some 8-ounce Irish coffee glasses, preferably with a few decorative green shamrocks on the sides.

When you are ready, pour the hot water out of the Irish coffee glasses and quickly shake out the excess droplets. Pour in a jigger (1½ ounces) of good Irish whiskey, then fill the glass almost to the top with hot coffee. Quickly stir in the sugar. Top with a heaping tablespoon of whipped cream, or maybe a little more for guests who don't have mustaches.

Ideally, Irish coffee goes well on a chilly night beside a hearth in a snug cabin, when you're in a mood to talk freely and tell the old tales of Eire.

If your Uncle Celty McConner or somebody dropped by unexpectedly and finished off your dusty bottle of Jameson's, remember that you can make a pretty good Irish coffee with a jigger of Canadian Mist. And, if truth be told, a lot of "Irish coffee" around the world is made with French cognac. But don't breathe a word of this to James Travis, upholder of Truth, Beauty, and the Irish Way, at any cost.

Befell it that, after the above text had been written, my wife and I enjoyed a visit with David and Eva Lee Hicks, who were opening a hunting lodge on the Choctawhatchee River. Hicks had a good selection of booze for this part of the country, and I was in a sampling mood. Among their stock was a bottle of genuine Irish whiskey and a fruit jar full of choice private-stock locally distilled moonshine that he had somehow obtained. I poured a little of each into separate shot glasses, and sipped of first the one and then the other. The Irish had the best of it.

* * *

If I want to do any serious drinking, when all's said and done, I'll stick to smooth bourbon on the rocks, but I'll have to admit that I do enjoy a cool mixed drink in summer as well as a hot toddy in winter. I have tried out, in the name of research, all manner of coolers and tall drinks, from Mobile Mules to Apple Knockers. The best of such drinks, in my opinion, are the various fizzes, made with bottled club soda and either lemon or lime juice along with gin, rum, and so on. The secret to making a perfect fizz is to have freshly squeezed juice and freshly opened, ice-cold club soda. Never use squirt-bottle soda or canned juice.

My favorite fizz recipe calls for sloe gin. Which isn't really a gin. It's a red liqueur flavored with sloe plums. The resulting fizz has flavor, bubble, and color. Refreshing. Inspiring. Inviting. Here's how to make a good one:

Sloe Gin Fizz

1 ounce London gin
1 ounce sloe gin
¾ ounce freshly squeezed lemon juice
1 slice lemon
club soda, cold
ice

Put the gin and the sloe gin into a shaker with ice, along with the lemon juice. Shake the mixture and strain it into a tall 14-ounce cooler glass that has been half filled with ice. Add cold club soda until the glass is full. Stir. Garnish with lemon slice.

Permit me to say again that a good fizz depends upon having fresh juice and live soda, and in careful attention to details. The same can be said for most other mixed drinks, | *174* and of course the place to get a good mixed drink is at home, not in a bar. Frozen orange juice is suitable for use in screwdrivers and such drinks. And frozen grapefruit will do for salty dogs.

My Aunt Bosey Lee, a normally unbibulous blithe spirit, believed that she had a recurring ailment, the name of which has escaped my memory. Whatever the name, it was soothed only by a glass of peach brandy. My father said, "Pshaw, Bosey Lee, a glass of peach brandy will sooth anything that you've got!"
Well, I don't doubt Daddy's wisdom, but choice of soothing syrups may be a metabolically personal thing, and, personally, I've never put much stock in peach brandy. For medicinal purposes tequila is my drink. In my bodily system, it's the only thing that will help a common cold, if taken along with lime juice and a touch of salt. It's a ritual, and is performed as follows:

The Tijuana Hoist

tequila
lime
salt

In your left hand, between thumb and fingers, hold a half a lime. Sprinkle a little salt just above your left thumb. Hold a shot of tequila in your right hand. First, lick the salt with your tongue. Drink off the shot of tequila in one gulp. Head back. Left arm up. Squeeze the lime half, letting the juice trickle into your mouth. Hail Maria.

Speaking of whiskeys, whiskies, and other spirits of high proof, I must say that the only time, discounting a bout with rum somewhere in the Caribbean, that I admit to having had too much to drink was at a wedding in Dunedin, Florida. My wife had been invited out to dinner with the bride and the female members of the families, whereas I was turned loose with the groom and a bunch of Irish uncles and cousins.

We were staying at a lodge on the edge of the Gulf of Mexico, and the upper rooms had a running balcony, with railing and outdoor easy chairs, the better to enjoy the salty breezes. After dinner, most of the Irish males took a chair along the rail and settled back. Just when they got started on their bottles of whiskey, Scotsmen started gathering in the parking lot, getting out of their cars in colorful kilts, with a walking staff in one hand and a bottle of whisky in the other. From Michigan they had come. And from New Hampshire. From Texas and Oregon. They had come to Dunedin for the Scottish Games, and, from the look of it, several clans were agathering. Further, many of them had booked rooms on the same floor as the Irish uncles.

Well, I'll tell you, the prospects of a quiet night beside the Gulf looked slim to me, and I thought that I detected a hint of panic in a lone observer from Thailand, who kept his distance from all.

I located my room pretty early and safely retired to it— but sleep was out of the question, what with the bagpipes marching up and down the stairs and around and round the balcony. The best course, it seemed, was to join in.

As the evening flowed along and the Gulf waters lapped on the breakwater, I concentrated hard on whether I was drinking *whiskey* or *whisky*, and with whom. Things got a little fuzzy after midnight. At high tide, I broke out my bottle of Jack Daniels' Black Label, climbed the flagpole, and let out a mighty Rebel yell that hushed all the bagpipes and settled all the wrestling bouts. At least, I like to think that's what happened.

In any case, the Thai checked out early.

TEA AND COFFEE

I don't know exactly how much coffee I drink every day, but I'm sure that it is far too much. I got hooked on it early in life, and I have sampled it all over the Western world, including some syrupy stuff that I had at various ports of call around the Mediterranean Sea, as well as down in Cuba before Castro took over. And of course I've tried various mechanical and thermodynamic methods of brewing coffee, including a steam-heated pot that we used on a U.S. Navy ship off the coasts of Greenland, Newfoundland, and other northern regions where a hot cup or two really hits the spot.

But the coffee that I've enjoyed most (which doesn't necessarily mean that it was the best coffee) was brewed on the banks of Roney's Washhole, which was a popular swimming spot on the East fork of the Chowtawhatchee River during my youth. After Saturday dinner, our first order of business was to catch enough "puppydogs," as we called spring lizards, newts, and such salamanders. We required about 50 puppydogs. Of these, some 30 would be used to bait "set hooks," leaving us 20 to re-bait with as we ran the hooks during the night. We kept the bait in a syrup bucket, which was a 1-gallon tin container with a wire bail, almost exactly like a paint bucket. After we had all of our poles cut and had made our sets, and baited the hooks, we took a dip in the washhole, if we had enough time. Before dark, we gathered up wood and built a fire. An hour or so after dark, we ran the hooks, taking off the catfish, bullheads, and eels, and re-baiting as necessary. After all the bait was used up, we made ready to cook our catch and brew some coffee. The first step was to wash out the puppydog bucket. Then we dipped up some creek water and brought it almost to a boil over glowing coals. At first sign of a boil, the bucket was taken off the coals, and a handful of coffee was dumped into the water. We let it sit for a few minutes, then "settled the grounds" by pouring a little cold water into the bucket. The coffee was great, and I still make it by that method from time to time.

I understand that broken up shells of chicken egg dropped into a pot of such coffee will also help settle the grounds. In any case, it isn't necessary to settle the grounds if you've got a good strainer. The packaged paper filters that are used with drip coffee makers are ideal, if they fit your strainer. In any case, don't actually boil coffee. And don't leave the grounds in the liquid for very long unless you want it to taste strong and have a muddy consistency.

The old percolators that you heat on top of the stove or over coals from a camp fire make some good coffee, put out a wonderful aroma, and produce a pleasant gurgle. Unfortunately, these seem to have lost out in popularity as more convenient coffee makers became available for the home kitchen. The automatic electric percolators may be good in concept, but in reality they are to blame for millions of cups of terrible coffee. I haven't torn into one, but I understand that the heating element is controlled by a thermostat, which in turn is controlled by the temperature of the liquid. If you put cold water into the pot, the electricity stays on until the water heats up. While the heat is on, of course, the water perks up through a tube and into a basket or strainer that holds the coffee grounds. The colder the water, the longer it perks. If you put warm water into the pot, it won't perk very long before the thermostat shuts off the heat. If you put boiling hot water into the pot, it will perk even less—and the coffee won't be strong enough. Some people don't understand this, even after I explain it to them, and continue to serve stained water for coffee. It won't work. Usually, people who have this problem are not coffee drinkers. If they were, they would find out what they are doing wrong, or they would switch to a more reliable system of brewing.

If you have cause to stay the night in a household run by electric perk people, and wake up in bad need of breakfast coffee, I suggest that you find a way to get near the electric percolator. Then take off the lid, pretend to smell the grounds, and quickly run a few cups of the hot liquid back through the grounds.

Drip coffee is quite good, if you make it strong enough. I also like the drip filter system. The only problem with drip units is that they never seem to get through. After mine quits snorting and sucking and hissing, it drips for a long, long time, or so it seems. When I decide that the thing is finished, it will let go with a series of steady drops just as I tilt the pot to pour myself a cupful. I suspect that the early morning mess made from drip coffee makers has strained more than one relationship.

I've also hand-dripped coffee through a tiny strainer into individual cups, and I enjoyed the results. I've drunk similar coffee in breakfast houses in New Orleans, as well as some made socially by a young lady who lived in a white house in Biloxi, Mississippi. She poured it in drop by drop. This is good stuff, but it is so strong and thick that a lot of cream is needed, at least to my taste. This coffee is not very hot to start with, and the cream cools it down too much. I have the same problem with espresso.

Cream and sugar are of course a matter of personal preference, and I like a good bit of both. Instead of sugar, I'll substitute a little honey, but, frankly, most of the sweeteners on the market leave a bad taste in my mouth. On the other hand, the various powdered creamers are all right. I had rather have a liquid, though, and one of the best is made from powdered milk mixed thoroughly in a little water, forming a rather thick cream. Real milk, however, is my favorite, provided that it is whole milk. Low-fat or skim milk is just too thin, and you have to pour far too much into strong coffee to get the right color. Real cream is too heavy, and might even leave circles of grease or butter on the surface of the coffee. Half and half is fine stuff indeed. Canned cream, or condensed milk, is not very good in coffee even when the can is freshly opened. It's even worse after the can has been open for several days.

Although I enjoy good conversation wherever I can get it, and I consider a coffee shop to be a very important part of any college and any small town, I really prefer to make my own coffee at home. Fast food places are hopeless as coffee houses, especially if the hired help puts in the sugar and squirts in some cream for you. Coffee from styrofoam cups is all right, but waxed paper cups won't do.

The more expensive restaurants will provide solid cups or mugs, but the service often leaves much to be desired. More and more, it's difficult to get coffee, cream, and sugar at the same time. After you finally get everything and mix the coffee the way you want it, with the exact color and exact degree of sweetness, the service suddenly gets too good. While you are talking, a waiter or waitress fills up your cup with more black coffee. What's more, they will often fill it to the brim, making it impossible to add more sugar or milk without running over the cup. Worst of all is the waiter or waitress who spills coffee into your saucer. When this happens, set the cup onto the tablecloth and push the saucer out of the way. Unless you prefer to have the coffee stains on your white shirt.

Instant coffee can be pretty good or downright bad, depending on how you make it. One criteria is that the water be hot. *Very* hot. The worst instant coffee I've ever tried to swallow was made for me, on more than one occasion, by a fellow who didn't let the water come to boil. He put the water onto the stove, and, while waiting for it to get hot, he carefully measured the powdered coffee into my cup, then onto the coffee he dumped a spoon of sugar, and on top of | *180* that he dumped a spoon of powdered Coffeemate. The result was a lukewarm mess, to say the least.

The best procedure, if you're making single cups of instant coffee, is to bring the water to a full boil. Put your measure of coffee powder into the cup or mug, and pour the water over it. Stir. Then add the sugar. Then stir in the milk or cream slowly, until you get the right color.

Some of the best instant coffee is made in a larger batch, in a pot, steaming hot. It is allowed to steep for a few minutes before serving.

I've always wanted my own coffee mill, but I don't suppose that I would use it if I had one. My reasons for wanting one are that, first, I truly like the aroma of freshly ground coffee. Second, I would like to experiment a little with various kinds of coffee beans. My reasons for not having a mill is that it's difficult to find a good selection of coffee beans these days, at least in my neck of the woods. There are about 25 different kinds of coffee, most of which grow wild in Africa. In fact, the very word "coffee" might well come from Kaffa, Ethiopia, which is believed to be the birthplace of coffee as a beverage. From Africa the coffee bean went to various parts of the Arab world, South America, Java, and other tropical places. Although it is generally held that the better coffees are grown at rather high altitudes, the specific kind of coffee may not be as important as one might think. Almost everything depends upon the processing. The beans must be taken out of a cherry-like pod, and must be cleaned of membrane and processed or dried in one way or another. Then the beans must be roasted—and the bean's flavor depends on it being roasted to perfection. Even slight variations can change the flavor. Of course, major coffee packagers will take great pains to blend the beans so that the packaged product will be consistent.

181 | Also remember that coffee quickly begins to lose its

freshness as soon as it is ground. It suffers both in flavor and aroma. For this reason, freshly ground coffee is best. Always. But modern vacuum packing processes keep coffee much fresher, so that these days most coffee is ground before it is packaged. Once vacuum-packed coffee is opened, however, it will quickly lose flavor and aroma while it sits on the shelf. This is often a problem with coffee brewed by people who stock it only for guests.

I usually mix my own grounds, using half coffee and half Luzianna. Luzianna itself is a mixture of coffee and chickory, but I don't know about the proportions. Some people add chickory to make their coffee grounds go further, thereby saving money; others, I have heard, use it as a complete substitute for coffee beans. Chickory roots are gathered from the plants, washed, and parched in an oven. Then they are ground up, and closely resemble coffee in color. I like the flavor that a little chickory adds to the coffee, and that is my purpose in using it. Further, I believe that a little chickory used daily helps maintain regularity. If it has any bad effects, I don't know what they are.

What about caffeine? All I know is that I want some of it early in the morning to get me going. Decaffeinated coffee no doubt has its place, and its taste isn't bad. But for breakfast I want the whole thing. I'm a fiend. I growl when I don't get it.

Hudson Strode, who taught Shakespeare and creative writing at the University of Alabama for a number of years, knew everybody worth knowing and had a photograph of Isak Dinesen 30 years before *Out of Africa* became famous in movie form. Strode fancied himself as a tea aficionado.

A tea party of sorts was set up when Bennett Cerf came to town on the last leg of a lecture tour. Cerf agreed to see three of the creative writing students, and Strode said that I could come—but, he specified, I would have to refrain from rolling my own cigarettes from Sir Walter Raleigh pipe tobacco. He gave me fifty cents to get myself a pack of ready rolls. I took the money. The tea was set at Strode's place, a beautiful house with a separate study and separate guest house, all in 20 acres of prime Tuscaloosa real estate.

One of the other students of sufficient talent, by Strode's reckoning, spoke a number of languages and had studied with Jesuits. He smoked Pall Malls, knew how to sip brandy, had read Ezra Pound in the Chinese, and could have taken tea even at Oxford. He was, however, in spite of a boyish face, quite tall and had large hands, like a basketball player. He looked rather ridiculous holding a dainty tea glass between thumb and forefinger.

I don't remember the third fellow's name, but, a farm boy with a flair for detail, he was very nervous and also quite tall. Cerf joked about having the basketball team for tea. I had slouched down in my chair and I don't think he ever saw me sitting there. About him I recall only that his glasses had lenses half an inch thick. As always, Strode himself cut an impressive figure, the way he stood straight and held his head up. I enjoyed the tea all right and made good use of the finger food. But the scene here struck me as being something of a cartoon, what with five grown men sitting around sipping tea from dainty little cups and talking about Isak Dinesen—who raised coffee.

Obviously, I don't have much advice on taking or making tea. On the other hand, it seems to me that the only secret is in having good tea, and then mixing it with water in the proper proportions at the right temperature for the correct length of time. (Follow the measures specified on the package.) In a kettle, heat some water to boiling, then pour it over tea or tea bags that have been placed in a china tea pot or other suitable container that has a lid. (The purist will probably heat the container first.) Cover the container and let it sit for 4 minutes. Strain the tea into cups. If you make more than one serving, be sure to strain the tea into a second heated china pot, or at least get the leaves out of the liquid by some means. If you leave the leaves in the tea too long, you'll ruin the flavor. For fear of bogging down, I don't want to wade deeply into the chemistry of tea, but I will say that flavor depends on three basic ingredients: caffeine, tannin, and oil. All three elements are released in hot water after 4 minutes. (Or, more correctly, from 3 to 5 minutes, depending on the hardness of the water, altitude, and a number of other factors.) If the leaves are left in the water too long, too much tannin leaches out of the leaves.

It is best to make tea in a suitable pot, but for convenience some of us will sometimes make it directly in a cup if we are using tea bags. For best results, pour the boiling water over the tea bag, cover the cup with a saucer, and let the tea steep for 4 minutes.

Some people drink hot tea straight, and others want a little cream or sugar in it. Some want both. Others want a drop or two of freshly squeezed lemon juice. A good deal should depend on personal taste—and on a knowledge of what kind of tea you have. A connoisseur, I understand, might take oolong tea with a little lemon or plain; pekoe, with sugar and light cream; Chinese green, plain; and so on. The list is long. All of these teas, I might add, are made from the same basic tree or bush. The three basic types (green, brown, and black) depend on how the leaves are processed. To a lesser degree, the climate where the tea was grown has a bearing on type and flavor. Generally, the better teas are grown at the higher elevations in equatorial regions.

My wife enjoys tea very much, and I bring her a new kind whenever I run across it somewhere. In recent years, I noticed that more and more herb teas are being packaged, and we have tried some of these from time to time. Someone gave us some store bought tea made from elder bloom, and we enjoyed it. I had only recently noticed about a half an acre of elder in bloom near a local creek. I gathered a brown bag full of the white umbrels and dried them for a few weeks. The tiny flowers turned from white to a golden color, and brewed an interesting tea of the same color. Like Mellow Yellow. We found that a fresh wild mint leaf in the cup, slightly crushed, adds aroma and helped the flavor. In short, this home-made tea is delicious and interesting—and the price is right.

I'll have to add that many folks who like hot tea don't specify "hot" tea. They assume that tea is hot. Others among us mean "iced tea" when we say tea—and I count myself among those millions. If I want hot tea, I'll ask for hot tea.

Although the brewing of iced tea isn't in danger of becoming a ritual, I might add that some people consistently make it better than others. The good flavor and color of iced tea are related, and both seem to depend on the water almost as much as on the tea. If your drinking water has lots of sulfur in it, for example, no amount of tea is going help it much in either flavor or aroma. But I'm not certain that the mineral content of water tells the whole story, for some of the best tea that I've ever drunk was made with water that came from an untreated spring. Some of the worst was made from city water in a town within 2 miles of the spring. The tea made with the spring water was very clear and pretty, and the tea made from the city water was rather cloudy. My nephew, who drinks iced tea daily, lives in the country near the same town, and he has pointed out, more than once, that tea from his well is better than tea from municipal water. Of course, I'm not advising anyone to drink untreated or untested spring water these days. What I am saying is that the water has a bearing on the quality of tea. So, you may want to experiment with various brands of bottled water that are on the market.

Forget about dainty little tea pots when you are making iced tea, which will be drunk or gulped instead of sipped. It's a great drink for hot weather, and some families seldom serve a meal without it.

Heat to boiling some good water in a small sauce pan and put a family sized tea bag in it. Turn off the heat and let the bag steep for four or five minutes. Put a scoop of sugar into a tea pitcher or other larger container suitable for holding and pouring liquid into glasses. Take the tea bag out of the sauce pan, squeezing the last drops of liquid from it. Pour the hot, concentrated tea into the pitcher and stir to melt the sugar. Then fill the pitcher with cold water.

Fill each glass with ice and pour the sweetened tea over it. Garnish with a slice of lemon, or perhaps a fresh mint leaf or two. I am especially fond of mint, and I crush mine slightly to release aroma as well as flavor. But remember that a little mint goes a long way.

If anyone at your table doesn't drink sweetened tea, it's best to make a separate batch for them. Don't try to make do with one batch of unsweetened tea, thinking that anyone who wants sugar can merely add it. This just doesn't work as well, and often results in a half an inch or so of sugar settling into the bottom of the glass. Iced tea tastes better and looks better if the sugar is thoroughly dissolved in hot or warm water before the concentrated tea is added. In any case, always sweeten the tea before adding the ice.

OZYMANDIAS AND OTHER VINTAGE WINES

Some people harbor peculiar notions about beer. My wife, for example, doesn't drink much but when she does she insists on beer from a long-necked bottle instead of from a can. Although I sometimes go the extra mile and chill a goblet especially for her, she still wants the beer poured from a bottle. The brand of the beer doesn't concern her overly, as long as it is "light"—which isn't to say that she doesn't have favorite brands. I, on the other hand, prefer mine "heavy"—and in a can. I'm looking at the economics and the geometry of the thing and, to some extent, the environmental consequences. An old problem in integral calculus requires the student to find the most economical proportions for a cylindrical container. I don't recall my exact figures on this matter, or the exact ratio of radius to length, but an ordinary beer can comes pretty close. If you don't believe it, compare the volume required to store a six pack in cans with that required to store a six pack in bottles. My wife won't accept the facts, however, and we usually have to make room in our refrigerator for separate six packs—one in perfect proportion, as neat as a sonnet, which will fit on any shelf, and one tall and inefficient, which has to go on the top shelf along with tall items.

My father, a man who drank more than his share of beer, also liked it from a long-necked bottle. Mostly, he drank it at home—always from a rocking chair beside a fireplace in his private reading room. Budweiser was his brand. He always left an inch or so of beer in the bottom of the bottle, because, I was told, he had formed such a habit while drinking corn beer during the years of the Great Depression. (Most corn beer, you see, had sediment down toward the bottom.) In any case, my father always sat the almost empty Budweiser bottles down on the hearth, where the contents were warmed by the fire. Thus, my boyhood adventures involved warm beer, and this might have influenced my belief that beer ought to be as cold as ice. But most real beer connoisseurs, I understand, prefer brew that isn't cold. Or so they say.

I won't go into the difference between ale, stout, malt liquor, draft, and so on, but I will say that my favorite beer, back when I could get it, was dark, came from Germany, and wasn't as highly carbonated as American brew. I've also had excellent beer in Cuba and Mexico. But for the most part we Americans are going to purchase beer marketed by well known brand names—which all taste pretty much alike, and all of which are at least dependable. In short, beer really doesn't pose much of a problem with most of us.

Wine is another matter. Sooner or later, every man is forced to sit down and take a sip of Aunt Jane's elderberry or blackberry wine. I've sampled this homemade stuff here and there all my life, including some made by my own mother, and I'm here to tell you that it's not good, even for a sip. Some of the sweet fruit "wine" sold in convenience stores isn't much better, and, to be perfectly honest, I've paid high prices for some wines with fancy names that left my ebullient expectation rather flat.

So, I'm not the man to give advice to anyone on wines. I have never had the time, the tongue, nor the purse to pursue wine connoisseurship. It's just too much. It's a profession. I can't even pronounce the names of some wines, and I've always been terrible at remembering the best years. This confession doesn't mean that I'm not fond of a good wine. I am. But I'll let somebody else shop around for it.

One problem with wine is that you have to use up a bottle soon after it has been opened. It's true that sherry, port, and madeira keep longer than the table wines, but even these lose character after the first day. Of course, the sparkling wines very quickly go flat.

But I do enjoy wine at my own table, as well as from my easy chair. Yes indeed. Not every day, but frequently enough. You see, I long ago gained the confidence of a truly cosmopolitan fellow who drank wine with every meal except breakfast, and at other times of day as well. This man, wise and honest in his foolishness, told me that his stock wine was American and inexpensive. He whispered the name, then sucked in his breath, as if he wanted to take back the words. I tried it, I liked it, and I have stuck by it for 25 years, winning friends and influencing people along the way. This wine is inexpensive. It's available. It's pretty much the same from one bottle to the next, which means that it is dependable. One year seems as good as the last, so you don't have to horde it in cellars. It's a red wine. Further, it doesn't have a cork to be dealt with—a fact that removes it from consideration by sophisticated folk. The name? Dare I say it? What will the critics say? It's . . . it's—I must whisper. No! No! I can't. I really can't. I'll put it in code. It's S'rolyat Ekal Yrtnuoc Der.

Merely having the wine at hand, however, isn't always enough. If you've got guests coming for dinner who might turn up their noses at such an ordinary offering, it's best to pour the wine into a fancy decanter and hide the original bottle. Put your corkscrew onto the countertop, just as though you had recently used it. After the guests arrive, sit the decanter before them, open it, and let the wine breath for a spell. This bit of winesmanship might well convince the company that you know your stuff, and that you are about to pour a truly worthy wine. If you've got anyone in the company who pronounces "France" to rhyme with "Fontz," wink at them or, better, get rid of them as quickly as possible. It is important that you never reveal the name or the brand of the wine. If questioned, just say that it is very hard to find. Unless you're in California, it is permissible to mention New York State. Further than that do not go.

Once I served my private stock of S'rolyat Ekal Yrtnuoc Der to a mixed group with a literary bent. There was a versifier or two among us, and I too enjoyed making a tight piece from time to time. After dinner, the conversation turned, quite skillfully, I might add, to poetry and William Butler Yeats. When a physically appetizing young lady, who worked in a book store, asked for my favorite Yeats poem, I picked up a copy of *The Variorum Edition of the Poems of W.B. Yeats*, which just happened to be on the table, opened it about midway, and pretended to thumb to an exact page. Without a smile I gathered my voice and started reciting, by rote, Percy B. Shelley's sonnet, *Ozymandias*. The few guests who realized that I was "reading" a Shelley poem from a Yeats book were too astounded to raise questions about my prank, and I got through the 14 lines without a bobble.

"That was just beautiful," the young lady said when I finished.

"Thank you," I said, quickly picking up the S'rolyat Ekal Ytnuoc Der decanter. "Wine anyone? Perhaps a loaf of bread? James Joyce?"

Shelley's *Ozymandias* is, I admit, the one and only poem that I ever memorized, except for a ditty or two. Actually, I never did set out to memorize the verse in the first place. I was taking English Literature at the University of Alabama, and the Professor, a little lady who had descended from the President Tyler or somebody, asked me, during a class meeting, what a certain line in *Ozymandias* meant. I didn't know what it meant, if anything. She lowered her pince-nez and told me to find out.

Well, I wrestled with and puzzled over the damnéd sonnet day and night for a week. I read up on Shelley and the | *190* romantics, and I even looked up certain words in the *Oxford English Dictionary*, thinking that perhaps some of the terms might have changed their meaning since the times of Shelley, Lord Byron, and that twittery bunch. Still, a satisfactory explanation for the line failed to come to me.

Finally, when forced to speak up on the matter before the entire class, I told the prim lady that I was terribly sorry but I couldn't determine exactly what the line meant.

"Young man," she said, stamping her foot, "If you desire to pass this course you shall determine its meaning."

"Well ma'am," I said, feeling that she had deliberately put me on a spot, "In that case I'll have to admit that in my humble opinion the line doesn't mean a damn thing." This statement pretty well shocked everybody, and I felt that I had to explain myself. "Look, ma'am, Percy B. Shelley wrote reams and reams of verse," I said, "and, after all, the guy died at age 30. He couldn't possibly have made sense with every line that he scribbled down, especially while trying to fulfill the rigid rhyme scheme without violating the iambic pentameter required by the sonnet form." Silence. The lady turned litmus red. "That's not to say that the line isn't important," I quickly went on. "It is in fact necessary to fill out the sonnet dimensions of 6 lines to 8, which, along with the iambic pentameter, makes a rectangle of perfect proportions, like a window pane, through which to muse on the outside world."

The woman blew her hearing aid and threw a perfectly proportioned 6 to 8 blue-backed book at me—but I got out the door safely. Several days later, after she simmered down a bit, she sent word to me that I could return to her lectures. I passed the lit course, barely. But I believed in my sophomoric conclusion at the time—and I still do.

Later on, I wrote an epitaph for Shelley, which, if I remember correctly, went something like this:

Bard thou ne'er wert.

The *Ozymandias* crisis rather turned my life for me, and I gave up all hopes of attaining the Ivory Tower. The thing even became a sort of life-shaping criteria, and I swore in front of more than one witness that I would never enter into a serious relationship with a woman who liked to read Percy Bysshe Shelley. I learned to spit out "Bysshe" while the words uncoiled. I might add that my good wife, an accomplished woman who is herself qualified to teach Literature, has never once read Percy Bysshe Shelley in the privacy of our home. At least, not to my knowledge.

In any case, I feel that wine connoisseurs and poetry lovers have a lot in common. A good deal depends on the cover of the book and on the bottle that contains the wine. Beer drinkers, by comparison, are honest folk. So be it.